Joan E. B_____ S__
June 11, 1984

# The Magical Art of Cake Decorating

# The Magical Art of Cake Decorating

**BY CAROLE COLLIER**

Sedgewood™ Press
**NEW YORK**

**FOR CBS INC.**

Editorial Director: Dina von Zweck
Project Coordinator: Ruth Josimovich

**FOR SEDGEWOOD™ PRESS:**

Editorial Director, Sedgewood™ Press: Jane Ross
Project Director: Marilyn Pelo
Managing Editor: Gale Kremer
Designer: Betty Binns
Production Manager: Bill Rose

**PHOTOGRAPHY**

Peter Pioppo

**FOOD STYLING AND DECORATING**

Carole Collier
Bette Friedman

**ILLUSTRATIONS**

Mona Mark

**DIAGRAMS**

Pat O'Brien

Distributed in the Trade by Van Nostrand Reinhold.

ISBN 0-442-28207-9

Library of Congress Catalog Number 83-51239

Manufactured in the United States of America.

This book is dedicated to Shane.
Welcome home, darling.

# Contents

# Acknowledgments

I am indebted to a number of people for valuable assistance in making this book possible: Dina von Zweck, who convinced me I could write it; Jane Ross, who placed her trust in my ability; Peter Pioppo, the photographer, and his energetic assistants; Bette Friedman, for helping me decorate the cakes and teaching me many new techniques; Ruth Josimovich, who was always there to lend a helping hand; Betty Binns, for her stimulating suggestions; Margot Ruckstein, for her nimble typing; Gale Kremer, for her helpful advice.

To all my relatives and friends who were helpful and supportive, thank you.

# Introduction

Cake decorating is one of the most rewarding of all kitchen activities. Those who have discovered the pleasures of home baking and decorating have found something deeply satisfying, almost magical, in transforming simple ingredients into delightful, delicious fantasies that sweeten celebrations and leave lasting impressions. A fanciful homemade cake is particularly special because it is a reflection of love and an expression of thoughtfulness, as well as a treat to eat. Sharing something so beautiful and so good with family and friends makes a joyous event become forever.

*The Magical Art of Cake Decorating* is a unique book conceived and designed expressly to help you bake and decorate cakes with style and ease, whatever your culinary skill. Accomplished home bakers will find an exciting collection of new recipes and cake-decorating ideas for a medley of occasions. Beginners, or those who have yet to attempt this highly rewarding art form, will feel as secure as a professional with the detailed step-by-step instructions, which are both easy to read and follow.

Be assured that cake decorating is not nearly as complicated or difficult as it may initially appear. Success depends largely on understanding how to use the special equipment involved. And the tools of the trade are, in fact, quite simple to use—and, for the most part, inexpensive to buy. In the first section of the book is a complete description of everything required with the use of each tool explained in detail.

While even the most experienced decorator will agree that the battle is more than half won by having the right equipment, the rest of the success formula depends upon the time and effort you are willing to devote to practicing the basic techniques. Like learning anything else, the more that you practice, the easier the task and the better the results become. In addition, you will probably have more fun learning to decorate cakes than you have ever had developing any other culinary skill. You will find that there is a special thrill when you discover how easy it is to pipe nearly perfect stars, flowers or even delicate leaves with just one squeeze of the decorating bag.

Although time and patience are the key to mastering the art of cake decorating, your busy schedule need not be a deterrent. A batch of buttercream icing that you mix for a practice session can be used over and over again, if it is tightly covered with plastic wrap and if the decorations piped from it are scraped back into the bowl before they have a chance to crust over. Stored in the refrigerator, the icing will stay fresh for a couple of weeks and will be available whenever you can spare a half hour or more to practice making flowers, leaves, scrolls, coils, borders or any of the other decorations outlined in the book.

It is important for the beginner to realize that although it usually takes many hours to decorate a beautiful cake, a project can be stretched over several days, if necessary. This book shows how the process of baking and decorating can be divided into stages to fit your schedule. Decorations, in many cases, can be made days or even weeks in advance and stored in the refrigerator or freezer until needed. As well, a cake can be baked and glazed on one day and then frosted on another. Whether you complete a project all in one day or pace it out over several, the results can be equally lovely, fresh and delicious.

Because organization ultimately saves a great deal of time, much of the planning has already been thought out for you. At the beginning of each unique decorating project is a precise listing of everything needed to complete it. You can tell at just a glance, for example, which decorating tubes and colors are required, how much frosting must be mixed and how many decorating bags and parchment cones to have on hand. All the necessary information is easily accessible to make your cake decorating all the more efficient and pleasurable.

Perhaps the most special part of this book is the cake designs themselves, detailed in the last section. They are sure to inspire you to learn the skills necessary to execute them. I have created a spectrum of cakes for every festive occasion: amusing cakes for birthdays and special celebrations; traditional cakes for holidays such as Valentine's Day, Easter and Christmas; formal cakes for weddings, anniversaries and engagements; whimsical cakes to bring to a picnic, cake sale or a new neighbor. There are even imaginative cakes to decorate for no reason at all, except to say that you are thinking of someone and want to let them know that you care. What's more, there are diagrams, patterns, large color photographs—everything we could think of to help you decorate each of them with ease.

But don't think that you have to recreate the designs exactly as we have. Being able to express your individual creativity is one of the greatest joys of cake decorating. If you don't care for the colors I chose for a particular cake, let yourself go and dream up some rainbows of your own. And, once you have achieved a few basic decorating skills, you will, no

doubt, want to start designing your own creations. You may have favorite cake recipes that you would like to use to execute these projects. (The cakes themselves are, of course, the foundation for beautiful decoration.) But, to be sure that you have at your fingertips cake and frosting recipes suitable for these projects, I have included a delectable variety of my own favorites.

Homemade cakes almost always taste better than those that you buy in a store. Because they are made in small batches with the freshest ingredients, cakes—and frostings, too—have a special lightness, a fuller flavor and an old-fashioned goodness rarely achieved in mass production. Not enough time to start from scratch? Don't worry. Packaged cake mixes can give very satisfactory results. (The types that call for the addition of butter, rather than oil, are usually firmer and better suited to home decorating projects.)

Whether you start from scratch or use a mix, I have included an invaluable collection of tips on preparing cakes for decoration, working with various frostings, even cutting, storing and transporting cakes to the party—everything you need to assure satisfying results every time you bake a cake.

Once you let baking and decorating become a part of your life, you will probably find it hard to stop, not only because you enjoy it so much, but because your friends and family will begin to look forward to your amazing creations. I know *The Magical Art of Cake Decorating* will set you on your way to letting them eat cake—and loving it.

Carole Collier

# Tools, Techniques and Tips

# Equipment

On the following pages are descriptions for all the equipment necessary to make and decorate the cakes in this book. In many cases, I have commented on my own preferences as a matter of interest. By all means, if you are used to or think you will be more comfortable working with fewer, more or different tools, I encourage you to do so. It usually takes many hours of work and concentration to decorate a cake, and it is essential that you be as relaxed and comfortable as possible right down to your shoes. A comfortable pair of flat-heeled shoes and loose, unrestrictive apparel will help to keep you physically at ease. It's also a good idea to wear a full apron because fat, chocolate and food-color stains can be difficult to remove in the wash.

Even if you have never decorated a cake before, you probably already have some of the utensils and supplies needed to create the cakes in this book. Some of the items that you don't own can be purchased in a hardware store or in the kitchenware section of a supermarket or department store. And whatever you can't find there, you can buy from a specialty shop or from one of the mail-order suppliers listed on page 22.

*Heavy-duty mixer.* Your biggest investment in cake decorating will probably be a heavy-duty mixer with a 4½- or 5-quart bowl. This is the only type of mixer strong enough to cope with large quantities of ingredients and the prolonged beating time required to make frostings light and fluffy. If you over-work a standard mixer, you will run the risk of burning out its motor.

If you don't own a heavy-duty mixer and don't want to buy one before trying your first cake-decorating projects, use a standard mixer with caution. Beat your frosting in a couple of stages and allow the motor to cool completely between each beating stage. Cover the frosting with plastic wrap while waiting for the motor to cool. For a large project, you might borrow mixers from friends or family members so that you can alternate and allow each to cool thoroughly without losing time.

*Mixing bowls.* You will need several mixing bowls of various sizes for tinting frosting. Two or three 1-quart bowls and about a half dozen smaller bowls should be enough for most of your needs. Stainless-steel bowls with tight-fitting lids are the best because they can't absorb odors, are unbreakable, stackable, lightweight and do away with the need to cover frosting with plastic wrap. For tinting very small amounts of frosting, I use the coffee cups from my dinnerware service. In addition, you will find it handy to buy an extra bowl for your mixer for those times when you have to beat egg whites separately or for when you have to mix more than one batch of frosting.

*Cake pans.* Most of the cakes in this book require pans of standard shapes and sizes. Those that you will need are listed with the directions for decorating each cake. I prefer shiny metal cake pans. In my experience, they brown cakes more evenly than those with a dull or dark finish. Glass pans or baking dishes will do a good job, but I rarely use them because they are breakable, cumbersome and heavy to handle. In addition, they bake cakes more quickly, and in order to compensate for this factor, the oven temperature listed in each recipe should be lowered by 25 degrees. Of course, if you already own glass pans and are comfortable using them, then there is no need to invest in metal.

*Wire cooling racks.* When a cake comes out of the oven, it should be placed on a rack to cool for about 10 minutes while it is still in its pan. When the time is up, the cake must be turned out onto the rack so that air will be able to circulate around it evenly while it finishes cooling. The cake must be cooled completely before glazing or frosting is applied.

The problem with all cooling racks that I have seen is that their short legs make it difficult for air to circulate underneath the cake. Steam escaping from the cake builds up between the table and the bottom of the cake, and you end up with a cake that has a soggy bottom.

The only way that I know to prevent this is to elevate the rack by placing books or cans underneath its edges. If anyone knows where I can purchase wire cooling racks with legs that are at least 3-inches high, please let me know. In the meantime, I can only suggest using the largest racks you can find, so that you can prop them from underneath, placing books or cans in such a way that the cake is not resting over them. And, large racks obviously hold more. It is always better to have more space than necessary rather than not have enough. You will need at least two racks, but it is even handier to have four. In a pinch, use a spare oven rack or a wire refrigerator shelf.

*Timer.* I would never consider baking a cake without a timer, because I hate having to watch a clock. Even though my oven has a timer, I find it convenient to own a portable model. Whenever I have to time something for more than a few minutes, I always set both, placing the extra timer at the other end of my apartment. That way, no matter where I am, I am sure to hear at least one bell when they go off.

*Sifter.* The sifting of ingredients plays an important role in cake decorating. It aerates dry ingredients, removes lumps and is necessary for accurate measuring. There are various types of sifters on the market, but I won't pretend to be familiar with all but one of them. Mine is a fairly simple model that has a crank handle, one screen, high sides and a 5-cup capacity. Although I often wish it were larger, it has served me well for a number of years, so I've never bothered to investigate others. Actually, I have two: one for sifting cocoa, the other for flour and sugar. I stuck a piece of tape onto the one that I use for cocoa so that I can tell it from the other. I think the reason that my sifters have lasted so long—this is a trick that I learned from my grandmother—is

that I never wash them. Instead, when I am through using them, I take them over to the sink, invert them and tap them several times to knock out any clinging particles. I store each in a sealed plastic bag to keep them free from dust.

*Measuring cups and spoons.* Accurate measuring is essential when making cakes and frostings, so it is important to use the right tools. To measure dry ingredients like flour and sugar and also soft solids like shortening, you will need a set of graduated dry measuring cups. Always level off ingredients being measured in a dry measuring cup with a knife or metal spatula. You will need two liquid measuring cups with pouring lips, one with a 1-cup capacity, the other a 4-cup capacity. In addition, you will need a set of graduated measuring spoons to measure quantities of less than ¼ cup. One set of spoons can be used for all ingredients. Always level off dry and soft solid ingredients measured in spoons.

*Rubber spatulas.* Your job will be easier if you keep several soft rubber spatulas handy. The narrow ones that look like half-spatulas are useful for mixing and tinting small amounts of icing and for transferring icing into decorating bags and parchment cones. Because of their narrow shape, they allow you to place the icing far down into the bag without making a mess. Buy about four or five, if you can, so that you don't have to keep washing them when working with several colored icings at once. The wider, standard size spatulas are a must for mixing food coloring into icing because they prevent the icing from sneaking away and accumulating on the side of the bowl while it's being stirred. The standard size spatula is also used for scraping the sides of your mixing bowl as you mix cake batter or frosting. Two or three standard size spatulas should see you through your needs.

A word of caution: Never scrape a bowl while the mixer is running. Stop the machine, scrape the sides and then remove the spatula before turning the mixer on again. If you should accidentally drop a spatula into the bowl while the machine is running, turn it off before attempting to retrieve the tool.

*Metal spatulas.* These come in several lengths, each suited to a different purpose. A 6-inch blade is a must for working on small areas of the cake, for transferring decorations onto a cake and for frosting the sides of one-layer cakes. An 8- or 10-inch blade is used for spreading frosting all over the cake and may also be used to smooth the sides of two- or three-layer cakes. A 14-inch blade is best for smoothing the frosting on top of a cake.

You will also need one or two sturdy pancake turners or angled spatulas with wide blades for transferring cakes from one place to another. When measuring a spatula blade, don't forget to include in your calculations the part of the blade that fits into the handle.

*Pastry brush.* You will need a 1-inch wide brush with flexible bristles for brushing away loose crumbs and for applying warm jam glaze to your cakes. The same brush can be used for both tasks.

*Knives.* You will need a few good knives for cutting and carving cakes into various shapes. I find that serrated blades work best, but whatever knives you choose, make sure that they are sharp.

*Scissors.* Just about any old pair of scissors will do for snipping off the tips of parchment cones, cutting thread and cutting out paper patterns and liners for cake pans. For cutting corrugated cardboard, you will need a strong pair of very sharp scissors.

*Decorating tubes or tips.* These are the metal nozzles that are used inside the decorating bag to form various frosting shapes and designs. The pattern you pipe depends on the size and shape of the hole at the tip of the nozzle. Although there are almost a hundred standard decorating tubes, and an additional array of special tubes to choose from, many have similar shapes and fit into one of six basic tube groups. If you are new to cake decorating, buy one or two tubes from each basic group. (See illustrations on pages 18 and 19.) The collection of tubes can then be expanded as you become more proficient and adventurous. Most tubes can be placed in one of the following groups:

*Round tubes.* These have plain, circular openings and are used for printing and writing messages and for piping lines, dots, beads, stems, loops and drop strings. Round tubes, numbers 1 through 12, graduate in size; tube 1 is the smallest. Some of the round tubes used in decorating the cakes in this book include tubes 1 through 4, 6, 8, 10 and 11.

*Star tubes.* These have tips with jagged, star-shaped openings and are used to pipe stars, rosettes, shells, fleur-de-lis and many more grooved decorations. Star tubes are divided into two categories:

Open-star tubes (numbers 13 through 22, and number 32) have short points and a relatively large center opening.

Closed-star tubes (numbers 23 through 31, and 33 through 35) have longer points and make decorations with more sharply defined grooves and edges. Tubes 49 through 54 have small cross-shaped openings and also fit into this group. Some of the star tubes used to decorate the cakes in this book include tubes 13, 15, 17, 18, 20, 22 and 32.

*Ribbon (basket-weave) tubes.* Tubes 44 through 48 are included in this group. Tubes 44 and 45 have two flat edges and are used for piping smooth stripes, bows and ribbons. Tubes 46, 47 and 48 have one flat edge and one serrated edge. For a ribbed effect, position the flat edge on the cake; for a smooth effect, position the serrated edge on the cake. The technique used for a basket-weave pattern is illustrated on page 39. Tubes 46, 47 and 48 are used to decorate some of the cakes in this book.

*Leaf tubes.* These have a V-shaped opening and are designed to make plain or ruffled leaves of various sizes with a ridge down the center and a pointed tip. The technique is shown on page 38. Leaf tubes include numbers 65 through 70. Numbers 71 through 75 are combination leaf-and-border tubes. One side of the tube is used to create fancy leaf shapes, and the other side is used for a variety of crinkled border designs. Tubes 94 and 95 are used for special ferns and leaves.

*Border and garland tubes.* These produce a variety of intricate decorations with defined grooves, ribs or ripples. Tube 98, for example, makes an interesting multi-faceted shell shape. Other tubes in this group include numbers: 62, 63, 64, 99, 100 and 105. Tubes 98 and 105 are used to decorate some of the cakes in this book.

*Flower tubes.* These come in a variety of shapes and sizes. Tubes 59, 60, 61 and tubes 79, 80, 81 and 97 are used to form the individual curled petals of different kinds of flowers. Perhaps the most popular flower tubes are the rose tubes which include num-

# STANDARD DECORATING TUBES

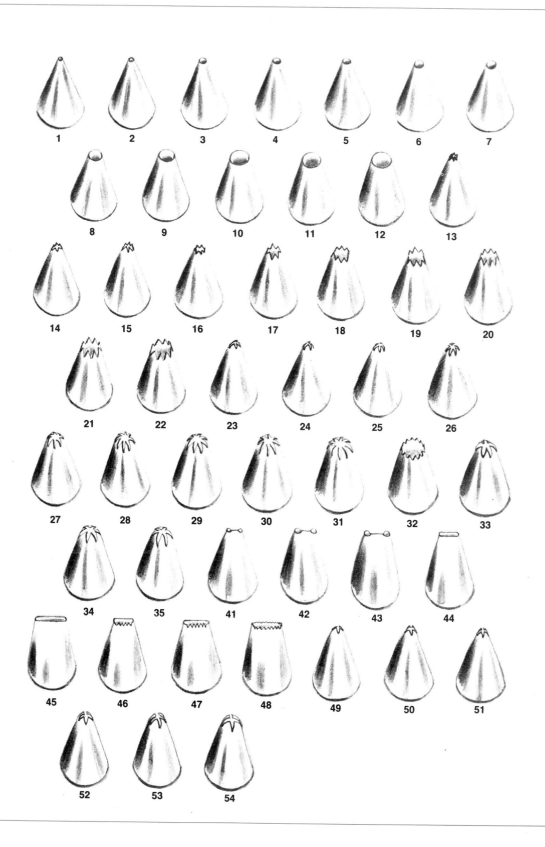

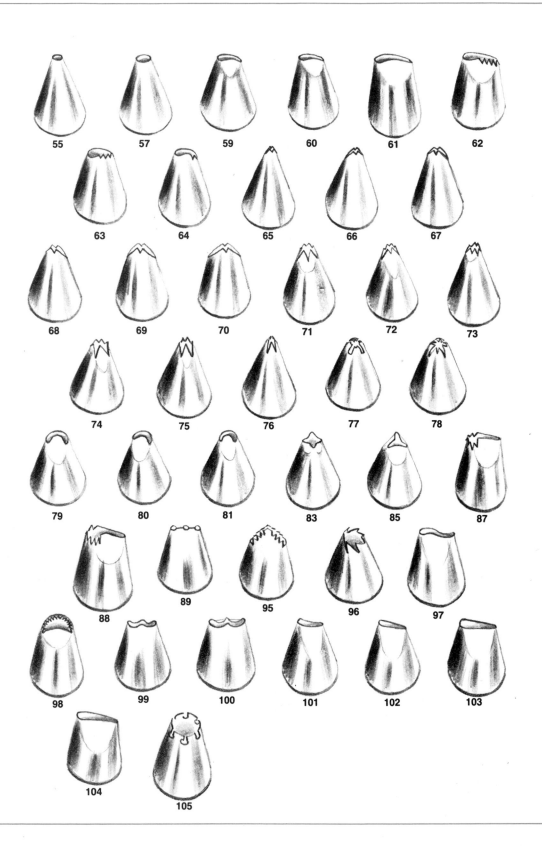

55  57  59  60  61  62

63  64  65  66  67

68  69  70  71  72  73

74  75  76  77  78

79  80  81  83  85  87

88  89  95  96  97

98  99  100  101  102  103

104  105

ber 101 through 104. They can be used for making rose petals and buds, as well as other flower petals. In addition, the flat shape of the rose tubes lends itself to making a variety of bows and ribbons. Standard drop-flower tubes that produce multi-petal blossoms with just one press and a slight turn of the filled decorating bag, include tubes 77, 78 and 96.

*Note:* Standard decorating tubes range from numbers 1 through 105. Tubes 36, 37, 38, 39 and 40 and tubes 90, 91, 92, 93 and 94 have become obsolete and are no longer available.

*Specialty tubes.* In addition to the standard decorating tubes, a large number of specialty tubes are also available. Many are simply variations of the standard tubes in smaller or larger sizes. A wide assortment of special drop-flower tubes is also available for making attractive flowers with just one squeeze of the decorating bag. Some of the special tubes used to decorate the cakes in this book include: Tube 65s (miniature leaves), tubes 124 and 125 (large roses), tube 150 (daisy petals) and drop flower tubes 146, 191, 225. A complete description and illustrations of the individual special tubes can be found in many of the catalogs selling cake decorating equipment.

*Tube storage box.* Made by Ateco, this clear plastic box stores tubes upright and in place for easy selection. If stored in such a manner, your tubes can't get damaged or misplaced, and the box is a good time-saver if you need to locate a tube in a hurry. It is not a necessity, but I would feel very disorganized without mine.

*Tube cleaning brush.* This wire gadget is only 3½-inches long; it has a tiny spiral bristle at one end and flat bristles at the other end. It reaches into the tiniest crevices of your tubes to clean out every trace of icing. If you squeeze a few drops of any lemon-base dishwashing liquid onto the brush before cleaning your tubes, they will come out sparkling clean.

*Decorating bags.* There are many types of bags available, and you should be attentive when making a choice. Canvas bags are very hard to clean; plastic-coated canvas bags, because of their weight and slight stiffness, can be difficult to manipulate; nylon bags, although easy to clean and handle, often weep when working with buttercream.

In my opinion, the best bags are made of woven cotton-polyester fabric, coated with plastic. They are lightweight and easy to handle; they wash easily, won't stiffen or weep, and their strong heat-sealed seams won't split or leak. Because they haven't any stitching, you can just snip off the tips of the bags to make whatever size opening you desire—small enough to hold a standard tube without a coupling, or wide enough to hold a coupling or a large special tube.

All bags come in an assortment of sizes. I find the 10-inch size to be the most practical and suggest that you buy about five or six to meet your needs. It is also useful to have one or two 12-inch bags on hand to accommodate large decorating tubes, such as the 124 and 125 rose tubes.

*Plastic couplings.* You will need a separate coupling for each decorating bag that you own. A coupling is a small two-piece gadget that enables you to change and attach tubes to a decorating bag without emptying its contents. To use, simply unscrew the coupling and insert the long, tube-like end into an empty decorating bag. Attach a decorating tube to the part of the coupling that protrudes from the end of the bag, then screw on the round piece to hold the tube in place. You may now fill the bag with icing. To change tubes, simply unscrew the round piece, remove the old tube and attach another, then screw the round piece on again.

*Turntable.* It's far easier to decorate a cake (especially a round layer cake), if it's placed on an elevated revolving cake stand. Professional models are the best because they turn evenly and smoothly with just a nudge and can hold up to one hundred pounds of cake. The best professional models are quite expensive, but they are worth the investment if you plan to do a lot of decorating. If you only plan to decorate a few cakes a year, then you can get by with a simple turntable or even a lazy Susan. I only recently acquired a top-grade model myself. My only regret is that I didn't buy one years ago when they cost far less.

*Flower nail.* Used as a hand-held turntable for piping roses and other flowers, this gadget resembles a long nail with a large head. Flower nails come in different sizes and shapes, which are distinguished by the number marked on the nail. The number 7 nail, which has an almost flat head about 1½ inches in diameter, is the only one I used to make the flowers in this book.

*Decorating comb.* This gadget, usually shaped like a triangle with jagged edges, each in a different pattern, may be made of metal or plastic. It is used to comb a neat, ridged pattern in the frosting by simply drawing it across the top or side of a freshly frosted cake. If you are working on a turntable, insert the comb lightly into the frosting at any point around the side of the cake. While holding the comb stationary, turn the revolving table around to etch the pattern all around the side of the cake. I only use a decorating comb occasionally, and as far as the cakes in this book are concerned, it has been used just once, to decorate the sides of the Della Robbia Wreath cake on page 101.

*Garland marker.* This is not a necessity, but a tool that comes in handy when you want to pipe a series of evenly-spaced garlands around the side of a cake. An inexpensive, adjustable plastic model should meet the needs of most home decorators. I used this type of marker to outline the garlands on the Sweet Sixteen cake on page 142.

*Cake boards.* You will need some sturdy, corrugated cardboard to support your cakes and to make them easier to carry, cut and tier. Cardboard cake boards are available at stores that specialize in cake-decorating supplies or by mail order. They come pre-cut in several sizes and shapes, such as round, square or rectangular.

*Paper supplies. White vegetable parchment* is the most versatile paper for lining cake boards and cake pans and for tracing paper patterns. Parchment paper comes in large rolls, available in 9-inch or 15-inch widths. Triangles for making decorating cones may also be cut from a roll of parchment, but you will find it much more convenient to buy a package of *pre-cut parchment triangles* if you are doing a lot of decorating. Parchment cones come in handy when working with small amounts of icing in a variety of colors and when only one decorating tube is required for each color. Parchment triangles are available in 12-inch and 15-inch sizes. *White freezer paper* is an alternative for parchment when lining cake boards; it is not suitable for tracing and I have never

used it for lining pans. *Plastic wrap* is needed for covering bowls of icing; the icing won't crystallize as long as it is covered. *Waxed paper* has a variety of uses. You can tuck 2-inch-wide strips of it around the bottom of a cake, if you are decorating the cake directly on a serving platter; the paper will help keep the platter clean while you work. Cut into small rounds or squares, it is used when piping flowers on a flower nail and for covering the open tips of decorating tubes when working with royal icing. It is used in sheets when piping many kinds of decorations in advance; just line a tray or cookie sheet with the waxed paper and then pipe the decorations onto the paper. *Aluminum foil* is used for covering cakes and for wrapping unfrosted cakes for storage. *Paper towels*, of course, are used for all kinds of clean-up jobs, and I use them continually while decorating.

*Masking tape.* You will need a roll of masking tape to secure the parchment when lining a cake board. If you need to use a double thickness of cardboard to support a heavy cake, you can also use the tape to wrap the two boards together.

*Thread or lightweight string.* Unless you are an expert at piping letters in a straight line, you will need lengths of thread or string to help guide you. Simply lay a piece of thread across the cake just below the spot where you want to pipe a message, and pipe the letters just above it, using it as a guide. Remove the string or move it down to the next line as each row of lettering is completed.

*Toothpicks.* Round or flat, as long as they are wood toothpicks, are just one of those little items that I feel lost without. When decorating, I place them into several shot glasses and scatter them around my kitchen so they are always at hand. I keep toothpicks by the stove and use them for testing cakes; I keep toothpicks by the sink and use them to remove dried icing from my decorating tubes. There are toothpicks on the table where I tint my icing, because I use them to measure out the food coloring. And there are toothpicks by my turntable so that I can pick off mistakes when the icing dries. I could tell you more uses, but I think by now you understand the virtue of always keeping a box or two on hand. No doubt, you will discover many other uses for them.

*Ruler.* You will need a ruler for making paper patterns, for measuring cakes and for measuring the height of cake batter in the pan.

*Art brushes.* It's better to invest in one or two good nylon or sable art brushes from an art supply store than to buy the cheap ones usually offered by most suppliers of cake-decorating equipment. Buy the type with pointed tips, not those that have flat bristles. A good brush is handy for repairing minor imperfections in frosting decorations and for smoothing together the gaps that can occur when piping long lines of frosting or when piping letters. Always work with a damp brush.

*Plastic drinking straws.* I use these in place of wooden dowels when tiering cakes, such as the Symphony of Flowers Wedding Cake on page 155. If I were going to decorate a larger cake than that, then I would prefer to use the dowels, which are much stronger. Never substitute paper straws for plastic; plastic straws are the only ones that can support the weight of the tiers, and they work very well.

## Suppliers of equipment

Cake decorating equipment may be purchased in cookware shops throughout the country, or by mail from the following suppliers. Catalogs are available upon request; a nominal fee is usually charged to cover the cost of postage and handling.

Maid of Scandinavia Company
3244 Raleigh Avenue
Minneapolis, MN 55416

Candy Headquarters, Inc.
"Tips n' Tops"
318 Main Street
Farmingdale, NY 11735

Cocoa Tree
12-14 West Marie Street
Hicksville, NY 11801

H. Roth & Sons
1577 First Avenue
New York, NY 10028

August Thomsen Corp. (Ateco products only)
36 Seacliff Avenue
Glencove, NY 11542

Madame Chocolate
1940-C Lehigh Avenue
Glenview, IL 60025

Wilton Enterprises, Inc. (Wilton products only)
2240 West 75th Street
Woodridge, IL 60515

# Techniques and Tips

It would be the worst form of deception to pretend that creative cake decorating is a "piece of cake." It isn't. But it is within the range of anyone who has a sincere desire to learn.

The techniques described on the following pages are relatively simple, and you needn't take a course to learn how to master them. At first, the results of your efforts may not be up to your expectations, but with perseverance and lots of practice you will be able to bake, glaze, frost and decorate a beautiful cake for any occasion.

So go ahead and read this chapter completely, then if you have never baked a cake from scratch before, you might want to start there in order to build your confidence. Even experienced home bakers should review the tips on skills such as handling, storing, transporting, frosting and glazing cakes. But the real challenge is the basic decorating skills—the means to a most beautiful end. Just try your hand one skill at a time. I know you can do it.

## Handling cakes

### HOW TO MAKE PERFECT CAKES

You can bake every cake in this book with ease, regardless of your expertise—if you heed the following tips. Experienced home bakers will undoubtedly be familiar with many of these tips, but not necessarily with all of them. And, if you've never baked a cake before, here's how.

**1.** First, read through the entire recipe. Make sure that you have all the utensils and ingredients required and that you are familiar with the techniques involved.

**2.** Assemble your ingredients and let them come to room temperature before mixing. Eggs separate better while cold, but beat to a higher volume when at room temperature. Butter should be soft, but not melting. Milk should be at cool-room temperature.

**Note:** Never substitute ingredients-different ingredients will give variable results. For example, all-purpose flour used instead of cake flour will produce a cake with a coarser crumb. If you use butter in-

stead of shortening, the cake won't rise as high. On the other hand, if you replace the butter with shortening, the cake will lose some of its flavor. Unless otherwise specified, the following recipes require large eggs, solid white vegetable shortening, double-acting baking powder, and lightly salted butter (not whipped).

**3.** Assemble and set up your equipment, including measuring cups and spoons, spatulas, mixing bowls, sifter, baking pans, cooling racks.

**4.** Prepare baking pans. To grease and flour pans, generously grease the inside of the pan(s) using solid vegetable shortening. Make a small wad from a swatch of paper towel and use it to spread the shortening evenly on the bottom, sides and well into the corners of each pan. If lining pans with parchment, place pan on top of parchment and trace outline of pan with a pencil; cut out parchment, then place it inside the greased pan and grease the parchment lining. (It is not necessary to line the sides of the pan with parchment, because these can easily be loosened by running a knife around the edge of the pan after the cake is baked.) Sprinkle one or two spoonfuls of flour inside each greased pan and shake the pan back and forth to cover all the greased surfaces with a thin layer of flour. Invert pan over sink and tap to remove excess flour. If any shiny spots remain, patch with more shortening and flour.

5. Prepare the oven. Place oven racks so that cakes can be baked as near to the center of the oven as possible. If using two racks, position them so that they divide the oven into thirds, and when placing pans in oven, stagger them so that one is not directly under another. If placing two or more pans on the same rack, make sure that the sides of the pans do not touch each other or the sides of the oven; air must be able to circulate all around each pan. Preheat oven to the temperature specified in the recipe at least 10 minutes before putting in cakes. At high altitudes, adjust recipe by increasing oven temperature 25 degrees. If using glass baking dishes, decrease temperature by 25 degrees.

6. Measure ingredients accurately. For dry ingredients, use a set of graduated measuring cups; for liquids, use a transparent measuring cup with a pouring lip; use graduated measuring spoons for both dry and liquid ingredients. Always level off dry or soft ingredients with the straight edge of a knife or metal spatula.

To measure dry ingredients such as flour and sugar, lightly spoon the ingredient into the appropriate graduated measuring cup, completely filling the cup so that the flour or sugar forms a mound at the top. Do not pack down unless measuring brown sugar. Using the straight edge of a knife or metal spatula, level off the top.

To measure sifted ingredients such as flour or confectioners' sugar, place a sheet of waxed paper on a table. Hold a sifter over the paper, then spoon the flour or sugar into the sifter and sift more than you think you will need into a mound. Using a metal spatula, lift the sifted ingredient from underneath the pile and gently transfer it to the measuring cup. Repeat procedure until cup is heaped full. Level off top.

To measure soft solids such as vegetable shortening or peanut butter, pack it into the appropriate graduated measuring cup, pressing out all the air space. Level off, using the straight edge of a knife or metal spatula, then turn it out using a small rubber spatula to wipe the cup clean. (Butter is sold in premeasured sticks; slice off the amount you need.)

To measure liquids such as oil, milk or water, place a transparent liquid-measuring cup on a flat, level surface and fill to the desired line of measurement. Check measurement line at eye level.

7. Time your mixing so that you do not overbeat.

8. Pour batter into the prepared pans and use a rubber spatula to smooth and spread it evenly. If baking more than one layer, use a ruler to measure height of batter and fill each pan equally. Pans should be filled to two-thirds of their capacity to achieve full rising. Cut through batter several times with a knife to break up any large air bubbles.

9. Use a central core when baking deep cake layers that are 12-inches in diameter or larger so that the cake will bake more evenly. You will need two empty metal cans to improvise a core. The containers from two one-pound vegetable shortening cans are ideal for this purpose. First, prepare the cake pan as directed, then grease and flour the outside of one can and the inside of the other. Place the can prepared on the outside in the center of the cake pan and weigh it down by partially filling with metal pie weights or raw rice. Divide the batter between the cored cake pan and the can greased and floured on the inside, filling each to the same level. The can will only take about 15 to 20 minutes to bake, so don't place it in the oven until 15 minutes before the large pan is due to come out. Check both with a cake tester before removing them from the oven. Cool the cake in the can for 8 minutes before turning it out onto a rack; cool the cake in the larger pan for 15 minutes. Loosen edges with a sharp knife; remove central can, then turn cake out onto rack to cool completely. Glaze both cakes, then when ready to assemble, simply use the small can-shaped cake to plug the hole the larger cake.

10. Set timer for minimum baking time. Do not open oven door until two-thirds of the minimum time has elapsed; if cold air strikes the batter before it has had a chance to rise completely, it could cause the cake to fall. When minimum baking time has passed, check cake for doneness by inserting a wood toothpick or other cake tester into the center of the cake; if tester comes out clean and dry, the cake is done. If not, bake 5 minutes longer and retest.

11. Cool cakes in their pans placed on wire racks at least 10 minutes, but no more than 15 minutes before turning out. Run a sharp knife around the edge

of the pan to make sure cake has not stuck. Cool larger layers for 20 to 25 minutes before turning out.

**12.** Place a dish towel or double thickness of paper towels on racks to prevent wire bars from leaving imprints. A clean oven rack or refrigerator shelf may be used for large layers. Turn cakes out onto one rack, peel off parchment lining, then place second rack on top and invert so that cake can finish cooling on its bottom to prevent the top from cracking.

**13.** Elevate cooling racks to prevent cakes from steaming underneath and acquiring soggy bottoms. Hopefully, one day someone will manufacture wire racks with legs that elevate the racks by at least three inches off the table. Until then, use a pair of books or a few cans strategically placed underneath the edges of the rack to raise it up several inches, so that the steam can escape from the bottom of the cake.

**14.** Cool cake completely, at least an hour before glazing, frosting or covering.

**15.** To store unglazed or unfrosted cake, cover loosely to prevent excess moisture from collecting. Insert wood toothpicks randomly over the surface of the cake, then place aluminum foil on top of the wood picks so that it doesn't touch the cake. Store at room temperature for no more than 24 hours.

## LEVELING A CAKE

Most cakes rise slightly higher in the center than they do at the sides, and I don't believe anyone has ever perfected a way to bake a perfectly level cake. If you are decorating a one-layer cake (depending on the design), you may not object to the mounded center. But, usually cakes have to be leveled in order to be stacked or to provide a flat decorating surface.

The most obvious way to level a cake is by slicing off its mounded top. When it has cooled thoroughly, place it on a cutting board, mounded side up. Place books of equal height beside the cake on opposite sides, and using the height of the books as a guide for your knife, cut a straight line.

Another method calls for standing a ruler next to the cake and using a toothpick to mark the cutting height desired. Repeat measurement around cake, inserting toothpicks at strategic intervals, then slice just above the path of the toothpicks in a straight line.

If, for whatever reason, your cake is still uneven after cutting off the top, tuck some of the top scraps (cut into wedges) underneath the cake at its lowest point to raise it up. Once frosted, no one will ever notice the wedge.

Breaking away from traditional methods, I have my own way of leveling a cake. I always fill my cake pans two-thirds full of batter, even if it means I have to mix an extra recipe. My cakes still mound in the center during the baking process, but the additional batter makes the edges rise to the upper level of the cake pan. Filled to this capacity, the cakes may require a longer time to bake. After the cakes have been turned out and cooled, I return them to the pans and slice off the mounded top, using the edge of the pan as a guide for my knife.

Cake batter should never be frozen. If you have batter left after filling your cake pans, use it to make a few cupcakes or an additional small cake layer. Uses for leftover cake are outlined on page 27.

## TO GLAZE OR NOT TO GLAZE?

Yes, by all means do! Before decorating a cake, it is essential to make sure that there are no loose surface crumbs that might interfere with spreading the frosting smoothly. Some cooks merely brush off the loose crumbs with a pastry feather or brush, but chances are that more crumbs will appear as the icing is pulled across the cake with a spatula, especially on freshly cut edges. I always recommend glazing before frosting. This important step not only assures a crumb-free surface, but also seals the cake, locking in its moisture and tender freshness. The seal works so well that a cake can be baked and glazed on one day, covered, stored at room temperature and frosted a day or two later without any loss of quality.

The simplest glaze is made by thinning about ½ cup of buttercream with a few teaspoons of water so that it reaches the consistency of thick cream. This mixture is then lightly spread over the entire surface of the cake and allowed to dry thoroughly, about thirty minutes, before proceeding with the frosting.

Better still is a jam glaze which provides a slightly tangy flavor that complements rich buttercream, marzipan or fondant frostings and offsets their cloying sweetness. Directions for making a jam glaze are given in the recipe on page 56.

## STORING AND FREEZING CAKES

Throughout this book you will notice that I always recommend glazing a cake prior to frosting. The glaze seals the cake allowing it to remain fresh and moist for several days. This is especially practical if you have a busy schedule and don't have time to bake and decorate all in one day. Instead, you can bake and glaze a cake a day or more in advance and decorate it another time. You don't need to refrigerate any cake that has been glazed. Simply cover it with a box or foil. You can refrigerate it, but cakes that have been chilled seem to loose some tenderness.

Sometimes it is easier to frost a cake in advance as well. Cakes that have been covered with buttercream will stay fresh for a couple of days at room temperature or for up to six days in the refrigerator. In either case, cover the cake with an airtight container to protect it from dust and other food odors. If using plastic wrap, insert toothpicks around the top and side of the cake to hold the wrapping away from the frosting. If the cake has been cut, shield the exposed area with plastic wrap, then cover the entire cake. Remove from refrigerator 45 minutes before serving and place the cake in a cool place. Otherwise, an extreme temperature change will cause the buttercream to weep.

Most baked cakes, plain or decorated, freeze well. The exceptions are cakes with custard or fruit fillings, which may become soggy when thawed. Do not freeze cake batter.

If cake is not frosted, first wrap the cooled layers in plastic wrap and then in foil. If covered while still warm, they become sticky. Place wrapped cakes in the freezer and keep for as long as three months. Fruitcake will keep up to a year. Thaw at room temperature without unwrapping. A single layer should take about one hour. Unwrap the thawed cake and, if desired, freshen it in a preheated oven at 350 degrees for about 10 minutes. Cool thoroughly before decorating.

Frosted cakes should be placed in the freezer uncovered until the buttercream hardens. When firm, wrap first in plastic and then in foil, trying to eliminate as much air space as possible without crushing the decorations. If cake is elaborately decorated, you might try using the toothpick trick mentioned above. Return covered cake to freezer and keep for up to three months. To thaw, unwrap the cake and place it loosely covered in the refrigerator overnight. If the frosting is allowed to defrost too quickly, drops of condensation will mar the surface. Remove cake from refrigerator 45 minutes before serving, but make sure you place it in a cool place.

## USING AND LINING A CARDBOARD BASE

Most of the cakes in this book call for the placement of a corrugated cardboard base under the cake. The cardboard may be cut several inches larger than the decorated cake and used instead of a serving platter when you don't have a platter of suitable size or when taking the cake to another location. The cardboard is disposable, so there is no serving platter to retrieve at the end of a party. More often, the cardboard is cut to the exact shape and size of the cake it will support. This is certainly necessary if you decorate the cake on a turntable and then afterward have to transfer it to a platter. Without a support, it would be risky business to move it. Similarly, when stacking cake layers into three or more tiers, each tier must have a supporting base, and if the cake is very heavy, the bottom tier might require a double layer of cardboard or a plywood base.

Grease-proof cardboard can be cut and used as is, but it is not as easy to find in a variety of sizes as untreated cardboard, which is widely available and can even be cut from a cardboard box. You can, of course, also use the untreated cardboard as is, but the cake will better retain its moisture and the cardboard will be more attractive and hygienic if it is covered prior to use. This involves placing a larger sheet of grease-proof paper over the cardboard and taping it in place on the underside. Because of its silvery sheen, some decorators like to use aluminum foil for this purpose, but the problem with foil, and also with plastic wrap and waxed paper, is that it tears too easily when the cake is being sliced. Heavy-duty foil is strongest, but it still doesn't compare in strength to white freezer paper or white parchment paper, which is what I prefer to use. The only cardboard bases that I don't cover are those that are placed beneath the layers of a tiered cake; the folded paper and tape would mar the surface of the frosted cake beneath the tier once it has been removed for slicing and serving.

To cover, simply cut a sheet of parchment several inches larger than the cardboard base. Place the base on top of the paper, fold the paper over the cardboard and tape it in place on the underside. (Masking tape, by the way, sticks better than transparent tape.) If the cardboard has a curved shape, you may find it easier to cut slits at several points around the edge of the paper so that it can be folded neatly around the board.

## TRANSPORTING A CAKE

The finished cake should be placed on a serving platter or board that is at least two inches wider than the cake itself. Secure the cake by spreading a thin layer of buttercream or a double thickness of damp paper towel between the platter and the cardboard cake base. You will need a cardboard box high enough to cover the cake and wide enough so that the platter or board will fit inside without being able to slide about.

If traveling by public transport, close and tie the box securely and carry it upright.

If transporting the cake by car, place the box on the back seat and prop it level with a rolled towel. In a station wagon or van, the box can be placed directly onto the floor. If you first cover the floor with a piece of shag carpeting, it will help keep the box from sliding while the vehicle is in motion. Drive slowly and carefully, avoiding pot holes and bumps, and try not to make any sudden stops.

## CUTTING A THREE-TIER WEDDING CAKE

The cutting and serving of a beautiful cake is one of the most exciting parts of a wedding celebration. The most disappointing part (next to missing the bridal bouquet) is being served a miniscule portion of cake that is barely more than bite-sized. Small portions are in order, but in my opinion, each person should be able to enjoy at least several forkfuls. The wedding cake in this book is a popular size, made of three tiers—6, 9 and 12-inches in diameter. It is traditional that the top tier be removed and frozen for the wedding couple's first anniversary, and in this case, the two remaining tiers will serve 76 modest, yet satisfactory portions, if cut according to the following diagrams. The top tier, if cut, will serve 12 additional portions, making a total of 88.

**6-inch tier:** Remove tier. Slice into wedge-shaped protions, as illustrated. *Yield:* 12 portions.

**9-inch tier:** Remove tier. Cut into quarters, then cut quarters into slices, as illustrated. *Yield:* 28 portions.

**12-inch tier:** Cut cake in half, then cut each half in half again, lengthwise. Cut into slices, as illustrated. *Yield:* 48 portions.

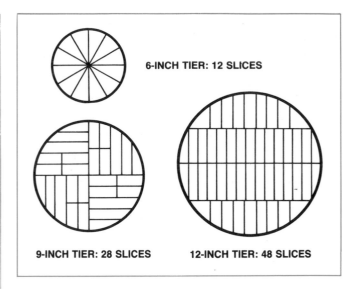

6-INCH TIER: 12 SLICES

9-INCH TIER: 28 SLICES

12-INCH TIER: 48 SLICES

## IDEAS FOR LEFTOVERS

Cake scraps and leftover frosting should never go to waste. There are so many useful ways to enjoy them. Whenever you cut discard pieces from a cake, immediately wrap them in plastic to preserve their freshness. If you don't plan to use them within a day or two, store them in the freezer.

■ Let your children try their hand at decorating. Present them with your cake scraps and leftover frosting and just watch how much fun they have. This is a great way to help them pass their time on a foul-weather day.

■ Try cookie cakes—use cookie cutters to cut shapes from a sliced off cake top. Glaze to prevent drying out and decorate with drop flowers made from leftover frosting.

■ Make petit fours with larger cake scraps. Trim the scraps into diamond, square or rectangle shapes, then glaze. Spoon warmed leftover fondant over the top of each, then decorate any way you wish with leftover buttercream.

■ Cut cake scraps into thin slices or rectangles. Layer with fruit, such as strawberries, raspberries or sliced peaches and whipped cream. Serve for dessert.

■ Use cake scraps to make a Zuppa Inglese. Sprinkle scraps with dark rum or sherry. Spread with raspberry jam, then arrange half of them in a layer in a large serving bowl. Top with a layer of vanilla custard. Arrange second layer over custard, and top with more custard. Cover and chill overnight. At serving time, garnish each portion with a dollop of whipped cream and a sprinkle of fresh raspberries.

■ Make a scrumptious chocolate-mousse scrap cake, such as the recipe on page 52.

■ Line dessert bowls with pieces of scrap cake. Spoon slightly cooled fruit gelatin into the lined bowls. Chill until set. Serve with a dollop of whipped cream.

■ Line dessert bowls with pieces of scrap cake. Top with a scoop of ice cream and chocolate or fruit syrup of your choice.

■ Present someone special with a gift of melt-in-your-mouth buttercream roses. Using tube 104, make roses from stiffened leftover Classic Buttercream. Air-dry, then chill until firm. Place each rose in a small paper cupcake liner and arrange them in a pretty box. They can be stored in the refrigerator for up to a week and taste best when served chilled.

# Working with frostings

### SPREADING FROSTING SMOOTHLY

When I first decided to take cake decorating seriously, I became completely engrossed in the decorations themselves. I spent hours at a time practicing beads, stars, shells and flower petals. I never gave a thought to the background frosting itself until the day came when I thought my decorations were good enough to place on a cake. Try as I might, I just couldn't spread the frosting as smoothly as I had seen it done on cakes displayed in bakeries or in photographs in books. It suddenly dawned on me that I had taken background frosting for granted. I used to just swirl it over the cake, but now I needed a flat, flawless surface on which to place my decorations. Fortunately, there is a way; it just requires a few tricks.

■ Make a habit of glazing before frosting. This assures a crumb-free surface.

■ Whether you decide to cover the top or the sides of a cake first is a matter of personal preference. The important thing is to complete the work on one surface before beginning work on another. If you try to cover too much area at one time, the frosting may crystallize before you have a chance to smooth it.

■ Use a turntable whenever possible to facilitate frosting a cake.

■ Keep your frosting covered with plastic wrap at all times. Remove any crystals that may have formed on the surface or on the side of the bowl. If you try to mix them into the soft frosting, they will appear as flaws when you smooth the icing over the cake.

■ Apply frosting with a long, clean metal spatula.

■ Always cover the area you are working on with a thicker layer of frosting than needed, spreading it as smoothly as possible. (I find that about a ⅜-inch thickness works well.) Even out the freshly applied surface by pulling the edge of a long spatula in one continuous motion over or along side the frosting to remove the excess. I usually sweep about ⅛-inch off the thickness. Repeat procedure, if necessary.

■ The secret of getting a very smooth surface lies in carefully stroking the leveled frosting with the flat side of a hot, dry spatula before too many crystals have formed. As long as the spatula is hot, it will easily glide over the area, slightly melting the fat in the frosting and smoothing every ridge and mark in its path. You must dip your spatula into hot water many times to smooth an entire cake, but you will be surprised at the excellent results.

■ Always work with a roll of paper towels and a deep jug of very hot water at hand. I like to plug in an electric coffee percolator filled with hot water for this purpose. It is sturdy, just the right size, and it keeps the water very hot.

■ Get into the habit of using a wipe-dip-wipe motion when smoothing the frosting. Wipe the spatula clean of excess frosting before dipping it into the hot water. This is important when smoothing the cake with frostings of more than one color. You only have to dip for a few seconds; the blade heats up very quickly. Wipe the spatula dry before applying it to the cake. A few drops of water won't hurt, but too much will make your surface streaky.

■ No method is foolproof, and if you have difficulty with the one above or still aren't satisfied with the results, try this little wrap trick. Smooth the frosting as best you can, then let it dry for about twenty minutes until the surface is crisp to touch. Lightly spread a piece of plastic wrap over the cake, and gently smooth the frosting with your fingertips. Don't press too hard or you will crack the crisp surface, and the icing will seep out and stick to the plastic wrap when you lift it off. You may get hairline cracks when using this method, but you will hardly notice them once decorations are placed on top.

## WORKING WITH COLORS

Colors are as important to a cake as they are to an artist's canvas, therefore it is essential that you learn how to tint buttercreams and icings to achieve various decorating effects.

Food colors are available in liquid, paste and powdered forms, and each medium comes in a broad range of colors. I like to use paste colors because they give brighter results without changing the consistency of the icing and can be used in varying amounts to tint shades ranging from very pale to vivid and deep.

What a lot of people don't realize is that there are two different types of paste food colors. The ordinary paste colors, of which there are several brands, often vary in texture depending on the colors. Some, such as pink and yellow, are soft and creamy while others, such as leaf green, brown and black, can be dry and grainy. The dryness is a characteristic of the color and has nothing to do with the freshness of the product. Gel-textured, paste food colors, on the other hand, are consistently creamy and easier to blend, but they cost slightly more than the ordinary paste. I use both types because together they offer a wider choice of colors, but when the same color is available in both ordinary paste and gel-texture, I always opt for the gel.

Paste food colors should be stored at room temperature and will last indefinitely if kept tightly sealed. Over a period of time, some colors have a tendency to separate and need to be stirred before use. To restore colors with a dry texture, stir in a few drops of glycerine. Never add water to paste food colors; it will dilute them and defeat their purpose.

Jars of paste color should always be kept upright, for if they are stored horizontally or are accidently knocked over, they may eventually leak and make a mess. A storage box with cardboard separators helps to prevent this aggravation. You will also find col-

oring a lot easier if you label the top of each jar (many manufacturers don't do this) so you can see the name of the color at a glance. Try to keep each color in the same place in the box.

Kits containing a small assortment of popular basic colors are available for beginners who otherwise might find it difficult deciding which to buy. With a little experience, however, it won't be long before you will want to expand the collection and purchase individual jars of more exciting colors. My own collection may be used as a guide and contains the following.

Gel-textured, paste food colors: sky blue, royal blue, lavender, pink, leaf green, moss green, mint green, forest green, desert brown, copper, orange sherbet, lemon yellow, egg yellow, super navy blue, super Christmas red and super black.

Ordinary paste food colors: orange, violet and malt brown.

I also keep a jar of powdered red food color because it tints to an unusual shade of strawberry pink that eventually dries to a warm shade of muted red. Powdered food colors are relatively new to the home cake-decorating scene. I won't comment on them here because I have been so satisfied with using paste food colors that I haven't yet gotten around to experimenting with the powdered.

There are quite a few tricks involved when it comes to tinting icing. They are listed here, point by point, so that they will be easier to digest.

■ Always use a clean rubber spatula or spoon to mix the coloring into the icing. If your untensil has even a speck of another color on it, it will distort the color.

■ When mixing a small amount of icing, use a toothpick to add the paste color to the icing a little at a time, until the desired shade is achieved. Be sure to thoroughly mix each toothpick measure of color into the icing before adding the next measure of color.

■ To color a large amount of icing, separate a small portion of it into a cup and use the tip of a knife to add paste color. Mix thoroughly, then add the colored icing back to the larger bowl and mix the entire batch together. Repeat procedure until the desired color is achieved.

■ When tinting icing, always mix slightly more than you think you will need. It is difficult to duplicate an exact shade of any color, and if you haven't mixed a sufficient amount to begin with, chances are that an additional batch will dry a different shade.

■ Tint icing during the day by a window where you can take advantage of the natural light. Artificial light from bulbs or fluorescent fixtures distorts true color and can easily deceive the eyes and sway your judgement of the icing.

■ It is always more appealing to decorate cakes in pastel colors. Dark colors taste bitter and can stain the mouth, so use them sparingly and for accent only.

■ Keep in mind that all colors dry slightly brighter or darker than they look when you first mix them.

■ When mixing bright or dark colors, such as red, black, brown or blue, make your icing and tint it the day before you plan to decorate the cake. Tint it a lighter shade than you desire because it will darken appreciably as it rests. Rebeat before using.

■ To offset the bitterness of red icing, add a pinch of artificial sweetener or a few drops of lemon juice.

■ Substitute chocolate buttercream whenever brown icing is needed. Use ¼ cup unsweetened cocoa, 1 teaspoon butter and 2 teaspoons milk to color 1 cup of white buttercream. Mix thoroughly, several hours in advance, because the chocolate will darken as it rests. You can always add more cocoa the following day, if a darker shade is needed.

■ Brown paste food color is actually a combination of many different color particles, and some of these colors take longer to dissolve into the icing than others. When using brown food color to tint icing a pale beige or light brown, mix and tint it the day before you plan to decorate the cake. When you are ready to use it, beat it again to disperse the slow-dissolving color particles that will have appeared as colored flecks in the icing while resting overnight.

It is quite likely that despite the wide selection of paste colors available, you may at some time want to combine colors to create a new color or one that you don't happen to have on hand. Mixing colors can be a lot of fun if you understand certain basic fundamentals. The results can also be disappointing if you have a certain color in mind and haven't a clue which colors to combine to achieve it. Following is a basic lesson in color-mixing.

The three primary colors —red, yellow and blue— cannot be produced by mixing other colors. Secondary colors are created by mixing two primaries: yellow and red to make orange, yellow and blue to make green, blue and red to make violet. The six tertiary colors are blue-green, yellow-green, blue-

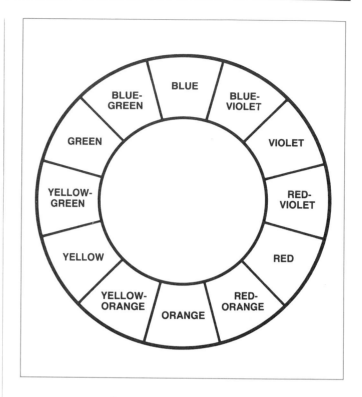

violet, red-violet, red-orange and yellow-orange. As you can guess, the tertiaries are created by mixing a primary and a secondary; for example, red and orange produce red-orange. You can also produce tertiaries by mixing uneven amounts of two primaries: a lot of red and a little yellow will make red-orange, a lot of red and a little blue will make red-violet, and so forth.

It is helpful to memorize the classic diagram that artists call a color wheel. The colors that are opposite one another on the color wheel are called complements. For example, the color wheel indicates that orange and blue are complements. When colors appear next to each other, or nearby on the color wheel, they are called analogous colors because they all have one color in common. For example, green, yellow-green, yellow and yellow-orange are analogous because they all contain yellow.

Brown and gray are considered neutral colors. A very broad rangle of grays and browns can be mixed by combining the three primary colors or any pair of complements in varying proportions. For example, various combinations of reds and greens produce a variety of different browns and grays, depending upon the proportion of red and green in the mixture.

This simple diagram of a color wheel contains the solutions to a surprising number of color problems you may run into when tinting icing and decorating cakes. For example, if you want to subdue a color, simply blend a touch of its complement (or analogous complement) into the original color. Such is the case when creating burnt orange by mixing orange with a bit of violet for the Wedding Vow Sampler Cake on page 152. On the other hand, if you want a color to look brighter, place a decoration tinted with that color's complement nearby to strengthen it, as is shown with the Hex Cake on page 64. One of the easiest ways to design a harmonious color scheme, such as for the Symphony of Flowers Wedding Cake, is to select three or four colors that appear side-by-side on the color wheel, and tint icing for your decorations using pale shades of these analogous colors. Then, to add a bold note of contrast, you can enliven the color scheme by introducing a few decorations made with one or two of the complementary colors that appear opposite the original colors.

It is necessary to study and understand your individual paste colors before attempting to combine them. Experimentation is the only way to find out exactly what colors your jars of paste actually contain, because most of them are tertiaries. You usually can't tell from the name of a specific color printed on the label. Sky blue, for example, has more of a green hue or a violet hue. The best way to find out is to mix a dab of the color into about a ¼ cup of white buttercream, then spread a bit of the tinted icing onto a sheet of white parchment paper and allow it to dry for several minutes. You can then study the color of the dried icing in natural light and let your eyes be the judge of whether that color leans to the right or left of its primary placement on the color wheel. If you want to tint your icing a truer blue using the sky blue, you will have to balance the sky blue by adding a tiny speck of a color similar to blue-violet, located on the other side of blue on the color wheel.

Some afternoon when you have about an hour to spare, mix a batch of buttercream and tint small portions of it using each paste color in your collection. Spread each tint on a separate piece of white parchment and label the paper with the name of the color. Later, or perhaps the next day, study each color and try to determine its composition. Write your findings in a small notebook, using a separate page for each color. Then, during the course of decorating, whenever you have occasion to mix colors together, make a note of the newly created color on the appropriate pages for the colors you combined. This exercise will teach you a great deal about color behavior, and your notebook will eventually become a valuable decorating tool. In time you will be as familiar with colors as any experienced artist and be able to use them confidently.

## HOW TO PREPARE A DECORATING BAG

Most decorating bags have a hole at the tip that is too small. You will have to cut it larger so that it can accommodate a coupling or a decorating tube without a coupling—the choice is yours. The coupling will enable you to change decorating tubes without emptying the contents of the bag. Cut the hole slightly smaller than you think it should be. You can always cut it larger, but if you cut too much off with the first snip, you may destroy the use of the bag. Just keep snipping a little at a time until the hole is just the right size.

Insert the decorating tube of your choice into the bag so that slightly more than the cut of its pattern protrudes through the hole in the bag. The tube should fit snugly.

If using a coupling, unscrew and insert the long, tube-like end into the empty bag. Push it part way through the hole so that the threads are on the outside of the bag. It should fit snugly. Attach a decorating tube to the part of the coupling protruding from the bag, then screw on the round piece to hold the tube in place.

To fill with icing, fold the top half of the bag down and, using a narrow rubber spatula, transfer a small heap of icing into the bag as near to the tube as you can place it. Keep adding small heaps of icing until the bag is half full. Unfold the bag, then twist the top to force the icing down through the tube. Now you are ready to decorate.

## DECORATING BAGS VERSUS PARCHMENT CONES

Listed in the instructions for each of the cakes in the book are the specific amounts of decorating bags and/or parchment cones required. When decorating, some people prefer to use store-bought decorating bags, while others prefer to use parchment cones that they have made themselves. Each has distinct advantages and I use both, depending on the type of task involved.

■ Decorating bags are stronger and better suited when large amounts of one color icing have to be piped, for the bag is easily refilled.

■ Because decorating bags are used together with couplings, they are best suited whenever several tubes must be used with one color icing. You can't change tubes with a parchment cone.

■ Parchment cones are disposable and easier to use when you only need to pipe a small amount of icing using one particular tube. Because of their size, they are also easier to control.

If you feel uncomfortable working with one or the other, simply recalculate the itemized quantity of bags and cones listed according to your own preference.

## HOW TO ROLL A PARCHMENT PAPER CONE

A parchment cone is a triangle of parchment paper that is simply rolled into a cone shape and used in place of a decorating bag. Pre-cut parchment triangles can be purchased wherever cake decorating supplies are sold. Waxed-paper triangles may be substituted for the parchment, but they aren't as sturdy, and I don't recommend using them on a regular basis. You might, however, like to practice making paper cones from waxed-paper triangles before investing in a package of parchment triangles. To do so, cut a 12-inch square of waxed paper into two triangles, measuring 12 by 12 by 17 inches.

1. Hold a paper triangle with the center point aimed toward your body.

2. and 3. Bring the right hand corner over, turning it under, to meet the center point (inside).

4. Holding the center point and right hand corner together in one hand, use your other hand to bring

## ROLLING A PARCHMENT CONE

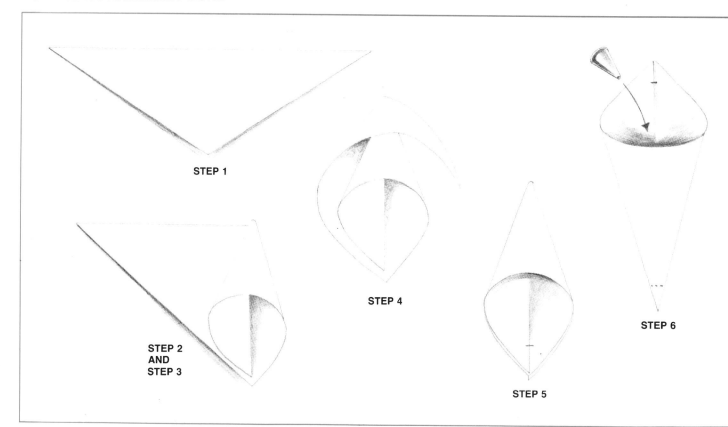

STEP 1

STEP 2
AND
STEP 3

STEP 4

STEP 5

STEP 6

the left hand corner over, turning it under, to meet the center point (underneath). You now have a cone shape.

**5.** Staple the joined points together to hold them in place.

**6.** Invert the cone. Drop a decorating tube inside the cone (pointed end down), then snip off about ½ inch from the tip of the cone with a pair of scissors, so that the tip of the decorating tube can fall through. Be careful not to cut off too much of the cone, or the entire tube will fall through. Aim for a snug fit.

**7.** Using a thin spatula or a dinner knife, fill cone halfway to third-thirds full with icing. Be careful not to overfill, or the icing will ooze out the top of the cone when squeezed. Flatten the upper (unfilled) portion of the cone, then fold in both sides of the cone as illustrated by the dotted lines.

**8.** Fold down upper points of cone, as illustrated by dotted lines, to seal bag.

**9.** Roll folded edge of cone downward several turns to form a handle just above the level of the icing.

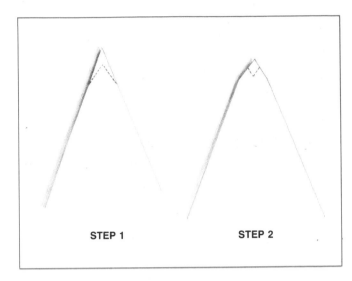

STEP 1          STEP 2

## HOW TO CUT A PARCHMENT CONE TO FORM A LEAF TUBE

Leaf tubes are available in many sizes, but with the exception of the tiny 65s, I find that leaves piped with metal tubes often split at the end, rather than forming a nice sharp point like real leaves. This problem doesn't occur, however, when leaves are piped from a parchment cone cut into the shape of a leaf tube. In addition, the cones can be cut with large or small openings to pipe any size leaf desired. I don't know who invented this simple technique, but the following diagrams illustrate the necessary cuts.

**1.** Make a parchment cone and fill it with icing. Squeeze the cone to maneuver the icing into the tip, then press the tip flat with your fingers to force the icing back about half an inch. Following the direction of the point of the flattened cone, cut along the tip of the cone to form a point.

**2.** Cut off a tiny V-shaped notch in the opposite direction of the newly cut point. Voila, you now have a perfect leaf tube! Fold the top of the cone to seal and form a handle, then squeeze to force icing through the leaf-shaped opening.

### DECORATING HINTS

■ When constructing a cut-out cake, always measure the cake before marking and cutting it up. If the cake is slightly larger or smaller than the measurements given in a specific diagram, you will have to adjust them accordingly.

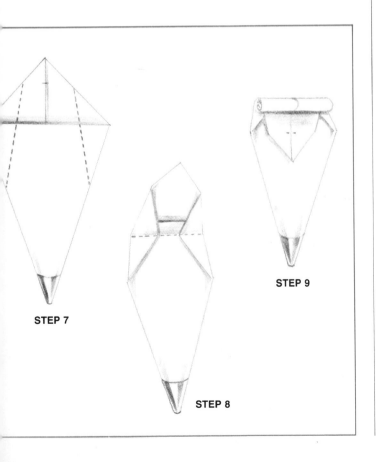

STEP 7

STEP 8

STEP 9

■ When making paper patterns, keep in mind that a cake will usually shrink about an inch in width once it's baked and cooled. For example, a cake baked in a 9- by 13-inch pan measures *about* 8- by 12-inches when turned out. The pattern must be sketched and cut to fit the size of the cake, not the pan used to bake it in.

■ To transfer a pattern design onto a frosted cake, puncture the paper pattern with a series of pin holes that follow the sketched design *before* placing the pattern on the cake. You will find it a lot easier to make the necessary toothpick marks through the pre-punched holes, rather than trying to force the toothpick through the paper and into the icing with one motion.

■ For a smooth finish, always brush away loose cake crumbs before applying glaze or frosting.

■ Rectangular cardboard bases sometimes have a tendency to warp or bend slightly when lifted. If you place a decorated one-layer cake, such as the Tennis Racquet Cake, on a single length of cardboard and lift it, the warp may extend through the cake and cause the icing to crack. To prevent damage, always use a double thickness of sturdy cardboard to support a thin or long cake. Cut both pieces of cardboard to the size and shape desired, then tape the pieces together and line with parchment.

■ Whenever possible, use a turntable to decorate your cakes. Place a sheet of damp paper toweling between the turntable and the cardboard cake base to prevent the cake from slipping while you work.

■ Practice piping decorations, such as stars, leaves, scrolls, garlands and so forth onto an inverted cake pan to get the feel of the motion before working directly on the cake.

■ To pipe words and phrases in a straight line, place a length of thread or lightweight string on the cake to form a line for your lettering. Pipe the letters just above the thread, using it as guide to keep them in a straight line, then remove the thread.

■ Keep an artist's brush and a cup of water handy whenever decorating. Wet the brush; lightly shake it, then use to correct flaws in freshly piped buttercream decorations. This repair trick works especially well when printing or writing or piping long lines. If the line breaks at any point, simply repair by gently stroking the ends of the break together with the damp brush.

■ Don't panic if you make a mistake when piping buttercream decorations onto a cake; simply keep the following toothpick trick in mind. Because buttercream dries to a crisp coat in a matter of minutes, allow the error to dry in place, then pick it off with a single toothpick or with a pair of toothpicks, tweezer-style.

■ Always transfer your cake to a serving platter before piping a border or caulking line around the base of the cake. Avoid platters with high or turned-up edges that might get in the way when piping the border.

■ To make a small cake look more impressive, place it on a pedestal plate which will give it added height. If the pedestal is very plain, you might even wish to tie a bow around it or add a touch of greenery for a prettier look.

■ When stacking a tiered cake, sprinkle a little shredded or flaked coconut in the center of each iced layer before setting the next layer in place. The coconut will prevent the icing from sticking to the cardboard base of the upper tier when the cake is disassembled.

■ Use a piece of very fine sandpaper or an emery board to gently file away rough edges on dried royal-icing decorations. File the edges of flower petals to make them look more delicate.

■ To store dried royal-icing decorations, layer them in a clear plastic box with napkins placed between the layers. The napkins will protect the decorations from chipping and serve to keep them separated; the transparent box makes it possible to locate various decorations at a glance.

# Decorating Skills to Practice

Cake decorating is a lot of fun once you get the hang of it. All it takes is a bit of practice. Make up a batch of buttercream frosting and try the techniques that are illustrated below and on the following pages. Practice beads, printing, writing, shells, basket-weave patterns, leaves and drop flowers on a metal cookie sheet. Practice border and string work on an inverted cake pan. Practice roses and other flowers on a square of waxed paper fastened to a flower nail with a dab of frosting.

To use the same practice batch of frosting over again, just scrape your decorations back into the bowl before they crust over. Keep the frosting covered with plastic wrap while working and when storing it in the refrigerator. Allow the frosting to come to room temperature before using it again. If the texture has become lumpy, beat it again for a few minutes. The frosting may be used repeatedly.

## Round tubes

### BEADS

*Use frosting of medium consistency and a medium-sized round tube.*

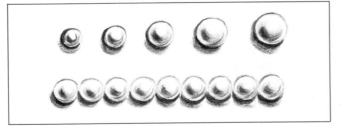

Hold the bag perpendicular to the work surface (straight up and down) with the tip almost touching. Gently squeeze the bag, lifting it very slightly as the frosting builds up into a mound. Stop squeezing, then lift tube away. If beads have points on them, tap them flat with a dampened finger. To vary the size of the beads, increase or decrease the pressure when squeezing the bag. Pipe a few rows of individual beads varying in size from small to large. Once you have mastered the pressure control, practice piping connected beads of equal size.

### BEADED HEARTS

*Use frosting of medium consistency and a medium-sized round tube.*

Hold the bag perpendicular to the work surface with the tip almost touching. Gently squeeze the bag, lifting it slightly as the frosting builds up into a mound. Gradually reduce squeezing pressure as you move the tube downward to the work surface, pulling frosting into a pointed teardrop. To make a heart, repeat the procedure, making another teardrop next to and touching the first.

### PRINTING

*Thin frosting with a few drops of milk or water, and use tube 2, 3 or 4.*

Hold the bag at an angle to the work surface with the lower edge of the tip lightly touching. Squeeze the bag with moderate pressure. As the frosting comes out, move bag slowly in the appropriate direction, depending on the letter of the alphabet or number being formed. As each straight line or curve is completed, stop pressing, touch the tube to the work surface to make sure the frosting sticks and then lift it away. Practice the alphabet and numbers 0 through 9, then try to pipe out words and phrases.

### WRITING

*Thin frosting with a few drops of milk or water, and use tube 2, 3 or 4.*

Writing with frosting is similar to writing with a pencil except that the motion of forming each letter comes from your arm and elbow instead of your fingers and wrist. Practice writing with continuous, flowing movements, being careful to form a series of letters in a straight line.

### COILS

*Thin frosting with a few drops of milk or water and use a medium-sized round tube.*

Hold the bag perpendicular to the work surface with the lower edge of the tube lightly touching. Squeeze bag and rotate tube in a circular motion. Use steady, even pressure as you continually repeat this procedure. To end, stop squeezing, then lift tube away. Practice this same technique with a medium-sized star tube.

### DROP STRINGS AND LOOPS

*Thin frosting with a few drops of milk or water and use round tube 2 or 3.*

Practice drop strings and loops on an upside down cake pan. You will be surprised how easy it is to pipe these seemingly fragile decorations.

Mark 2-inch intervals around the top edge of the cake pan with dots of frosting. Hold the bag level with the top edge of the pan with the tip touching one of the frosting dots. Squeeze the bag, making sure that the frosting sticks to the marked dot, and using constant pressure, pull the tube straight out toward yourself and then over to the next marked dot. Do not lower the tube; the string will drop by itself. Relax pressure and touch the tube to the mark so that the string of frosting sticks. Stop pressure, then lift tube away. To make loops, repeat the above procedure, but return to the starting mark after pulling string outward. Practice making single drop strings and loops until you gain confidence, then try a more complicated pattern, such as the one shown here.

## Star tubes

### STARS

*Use frosting of medium consistency and star tube 19, 20 or 21.*

Hold the bag perpendicular to the work surface with the tip almost touching. Squeeze the bag without lifting it, until the frosting forms a star. Stop squeezing, then lift tube straight up and away. To vary the size of the stars, increase or decrease the pressure when squeezing the bag. This procedure may also be used with any of the special drop flower tubes.

## ROSETTES

*Use frosting of medium consistency and star tube 19, 20 or 21.*

Rosettes are made just like stars but twist the tube around in a circular motion as you squeeze the bag. Stop pressure before lifting the tube away. This procedure may also be used with any of the special drop flower tubes.

## FULL SHELLS

*Use frosting of medium consistency and star tube 19, 20 or 21.*

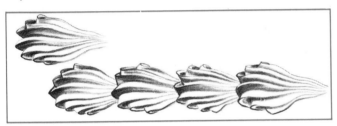

Hold the bag at an angle to the work surface with the lower edge of the tip lightly touching. Squeeze the bag firmly, lifting the tube slightly so that the frosting builds into a full mound. Relax pressure slightly as you pull the tube downward and to the surface, forming a pointed tail. Stop squeezing, then pull tube away. Always work toward yourself when making shells. To connect, begin the next shell immediately behind and over the tail of the first one.

## CURVED SHELLS

Curved shells are made just like the full shells (above) but curve the tube to one side (left or right) as the frosting builds to form a mound. Relax pressure slightly as you pull the tube downward to form a pointed tail. Stop squeezing, then pull tube away.

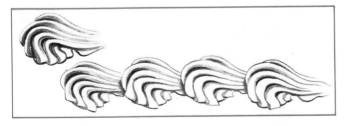

## REVERSE SHELLS

A border of reverse shells is made by connecting a series of curved shells that twist in opposite directions. Practice connecting a right curved shell to a left curved shell, and so on.

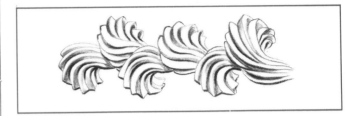

## STAR HEARTS

*Use frosting of medium consistency and star tube of your choice.*

Make an upright curved shell, slanting its tail at an angle. To form a heart, repeat procedure but curve second shell in the opposite direction so that the heads of both shells bow toward each other with tails joining.

## FLEUR-DE-LIS

*Use frosting of medium consistency and star tube 19, 20 or 21.*

Make an upright full shell. Just to the left of the shell, make a curved shell overlapping its pointed tail on the tail of the center shell. Repeat the procedure for the right side of the decoration. If desired, use a medium-sized round tube to make a ball at the tip of the fleur-de-lis tail.

### SCROLLS

*Use frosting of medium consistency and star tube 19, 20 or 21.*

Hold the bag perpendicular to the work surface with the tip almost touching. Squeeze bag until frosting forms a star, and using steady, even pressure pull the tube along in an elongated S motion. To end, twist tube slightly to form a rosette, stop squeezing, then lift tube away.

# Leaf tubes

### PLAIN LEAVES

*Use frosting of medium consistency and a medium-sized leaf tube.*

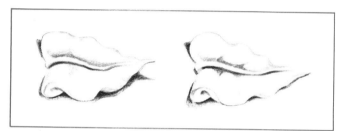

Hold bag at an angle to the work surface with the lower edge of the tip lightly touching. Squeeze with firm pressure so that the frosting fans into a wide base, and then relax pressure as you pull the tube away, slowly raising and lowering it to form a gracefully curved leaf. Stop squeezing, then remove tube.

When piping leaves, you may have a problem with getting them to finish in a nice sharp point. This may be due to a manufacturing problem. When the tube is cut on the machine, a small burr or rough edge is sometimes left on the inside of the tube. It is actually this burr that causes leaves to split at the ends. To correct the problem, simply use a nail file to smooth the inside edge of the tip. Otherwise, you might try piping leaves through a parchment cone that has been cut into the shape of a leaf tube. The cutting method is described and illustrated on page 33.

### FERNS

*Thin frosting with a few drops of milk or water, and use a medium-sized leaf tube.*

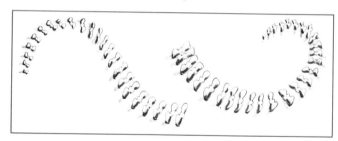

Hold the bag perpendicular to the work surface with the tip lightly touching. Squeeze out a small amount of frosting, stop pressure, pull tube away. Repeat this procedure several times, leaving a small space in between each leaf impression.

# Ribbon or basket-weave tubes

### RUFFLES

*Use frosting of medium consistency and tube 46 or 47.*

Hold the bag at an angle to the work surface with the lower edge of the tip lightly touching. Using steady, even pressure, move the tube in a straight line across the work surface, raising and lowering it to form a long ruffle.

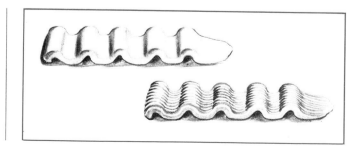

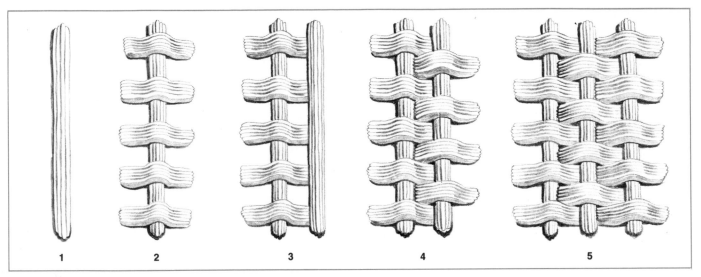

## BASKET WEAVE

To end, stop squeezing on a downward motion, then lift the tube away. For a smooth effect, practice with the serrated edge of the tube toward the work surface; for a ribbed effect, reverse the edge of the tube.

### BASKET WEAVE

*Use frosting of medium consistency.*

Fit two decorating bags with couplings. Fill one bag with white buttercream and attach a medium-sized round or star tube, for example, number 5 or number 17. Fill the other bag with yellow buttercream and attach tube 47. Practice basket-weave pattern on an inverted cake pan.

1. With bag of white buttercream, pipe a vertical line down the side of the cake pan from top to bottom.

2. Switch to bag of yellow buttercream, and hold tube so that the serrated side faces outward. Cover the length of the vertical line with tube 47 horizontal slats, piping them a tube width apart.

3. Pipe another white vertical line a short distance from the first so that its path just overlaps the tips of the horizontal slats.

4. Cover the second vertical line with more horizontal slats piping them into the spaces created by the previous row of slats. Continue procedure until entire side of cake pan is covered in a woven basket-weave pattern. See Basket of Daisies cake on page 90 and Strawberry Basket cake on page 74.

# Border and garland tubes

*Use frosting of medium consistency when piping borders or garlands.*

### ZIGZAGS

Using tube 98 or 105, hold bag at an angle to the work surface with the tip lightly touching. Squeeze bag with steady, even pressure, moving the tube in a side-to-side wavy motion as you pull it along. To end, stop pressure, then pull tube away. Star tubes also make attractive zigzag borders.

### GARLANDS

Practice garlands on an upside down cake pan using one of the border and garland tubes listed on page 17. Mark 3-inch intervals around the top edge of the cake pan with dots of frosting. Hold the bag so that it is level with the top edge of the pan and the tip is touching one of the frosting dots. Squeeze the bag using a shell, ruffle or zigzag motion as you draw the tube in a curved line on the side of the cake pan and over to the next mark. Repeat procedure around pan.

# Making flowers

### BASIC FLOWER PETALS

Many flowers, including pale pink or white apple-blossoms, yellow buttercups, blue forget-me-nots, pink impatiens and violets, have the same basic petal shape. Practice the simple petal technique below to make an assortment of darling blossoms simply by varying the color and size of the petals.

*Fit a coupling to a decorating bag. Fill bag with icing and attach tube 101, 102, 103 or 104. Cut a sheet of waxed paper into 2-inch squares.*

1. Attach a waxed-paper square to a flower nail with a dab of icing. Hold bag at an angle almost parallel to the nail's surface with the wide end of the tube touching the nail center and the narrow end pointed outward and slightly raised. The more you raise the narrow end, the more cupped the petal. Squeeze bag and slowly turn nail while you move tube toward the edge of the nail and back again to the center. Reduce pressure as you return to the starting point, then stop pressure and lift tube away. Note that the size of the petal is not only determined by the tube number, but also by the distance the tube is moved outward from the center of the nail. Practice making short and long petals with each tube 101 through 104 until you gain confidence with the technique.

2. On a fresh waxed-paper square, pipe five petals of equal size to form a flower. Pipe a small round-tube dot in the center with a different color icing as a final touch.

3. To make a ruffled petal, start with a fresh waxed-paper square. Use the petal technique above, but add a back and forth hand motion as you move the tube outward and back to the starting point. Pipe five petals of equal size to form a flower. Finish with a small round-tube dot in the center.

4. If desired, use an artist's brush to paint details on the flowers with diluted liquid or paste food coloring. Flower centers can be shaded with a contrasting or darker color, or the edges of the petals can be painted a deeper shade.

5. Air-dry royal-icing flowers overnight. When dry and firm, peel off waxed paper and store the flowers in an air-tight container for future use. They will keep for many months. Flowers made with buttercream should be air-dried and placed in the refrigerator until thoroughly chilled before attempting to remove the waxed paper.

### VIOLETS

*Attach tube 59 to a decorating bag filled with violet icing. Cut a sheet of waxed paper into 2-inch squares.*

1. Attach a waxed paper square to a flower nail with a dab of icing. Using basic smooth-petal technique, pipe two small petals about ¼-inch long.

2. Using the same tube, pipe three slightly longer

petals opposite the first two. Transfer paper with violet to a tray and repeat procedure to make another violet.

3. When you have finished making your violets, attach tube 2 to a decorating bag containing a small amount of yellow icing. Pipe two dots in the center of each violet.

### PANSIES

*Fit two decorating bags with couplings. Fill one bag with pale lemon-yellow or pale violet icing and attach tube 60. Fill the other bag with violet icing and attach tube 61. Set aside a small amount of white icing covered with plastic wrap. Cut a sheet of waxed paper into 3-inch squares.*

1. Squeeze a dab of icing onto a flower nail and attach a waxed paper square. Hold bag of violet icing at an angle almost parallel to the nail's surface with the wide end of the tube touching the nail center and the narrow end pointed out and slightly raised. Squeeze bag and turn nail slightly while you move tube out about ⅝ inch toward the edge of the nail and then back again to form a loop-shape petal. Reduce pressure as you return to starting point, then stop pressure and lift tube away. Form a second petal next to the first.

2. Switch to the bag of pale icing, and squeeze out a wide bottom petal, using a back and forth motion for a ruffled effect.

3. Continuing with the bag of pale icing and the looped petal movements, pipe two shorter petals on top of the violet petals. Transfer paper with flower to a tray, and repeat procedures to form another pansy.

4. When you have finished making the flowers, use an artist's brush to paint thinned violet icing in the center of each. With the reserved white icing, pipe two white dots in the center of each flower using tube 2.

### FORSYTHIA BLOSSOMS

*Attach tube 101 to a decorating bag filled with lemon-yellow buttercream or royal icing. Buttercream flowers should be piped directly onto cake, royal-icing flowers onto a sheet of waxed paper placed on a tray for support.*

1. Hold bag perpendicular to the work surface with the wide end of the tube touching the surface and pointed toward yourself and the narrow end of the tube slightly raised and pointed away. To make center petal, squeeze bag, lifting it slightly as you move it about ¼ inch toward yourself then gradually decrease pressure, bringing it downward for another ¼ inch. Stop pressure, lift tube away.

2. Use same method, curving the tube slightly, to make a right petal and then a left one. Air-dry royal-icing flowers overnight. To position on cake, pipe a tube 4 tan-colored stem where desired and arrange blossoms on both sides of the stem. Finish by piping two tube 65s green leaves at the base of each blossom, attaching the leaves to the stem. See the Easter Egg cake on page 88.

### SWEET PEAS

*Fit a decorating bag with a coupling, and using an artist's brush or a spatula, paint a ¼-inch wide stripe of pink paste food color inside the bag from the base almost to the top edge. Fill bag with very pale pink or white icing, and attach tube 103. Turn tube so that narrow end is in line with the pink stripe. Cut a sheet of waxed paper into 3-inch squares.*

1. Attach a paper square to a flower nail with a dab of icing. Using basic ruffled-petal technique, pipe one continuous ruffled petal around the nail in a

horseshoe shape. (You may have to pipe several flowers before the pink trim begins to appear at the outer edge of the ruffled petal.)

2. Now, holding the tube perpendicular to the nail's surface with the narrow end slightly raised above the ruffled petal (about ⅜ inch from the edge) and the wide end touching the opening of the horseshoe shape, proceed to make a central petal as described for the forsythia blossoms above.

3. Pipe two more forsythia-type petals on either side of the central petal, curving them so that all three petals join at the top and the bottom.

### NARCISSUS

*Fit two decorating bags with couplings. Fill one bag with white icing and attach tube 102 or 103. Half fill the other bag with yellow-orange icing and attach tube 2. Cut a sheet of waxed paper into 3-inch squares.*

1. Attach a paper square to a flower nail with a dab of icing. Using white icing and the basic smooth petal technique, pipe six ¾-inch long petals, overlapping slightly to fit.

2. With yellow-orange icing, pipe two or three string circles about ¼ inch in diameter, one on top of the other, to form the center of the flower.

3. Dust your fingers with cornstarch or confectioners' sugar, and carefully pinch each petal into a point.

### DAISIES

*Fit two decorating bags with couplings. Fill one bag with white icing and attach tube 150. Fill the other bag with lemon-yellow icing and attach tube 8. Cut a sheet of waxed paper into 3-inch squares.*

1. Squeeze a dab of yellow icing onto a flower nail and attach one of the paper squares. Pipe a large, tube 8 bead about ⅜ inch in diameter onto the center of the paper. If the bead is pointed, tap it flat with a dampened finger.

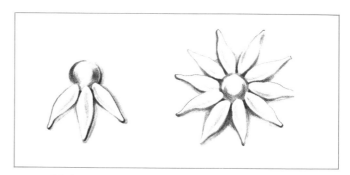

2. Hold bag of white icing over and perpendicular to the nail's surface with one end of the tube almost touching the edge of the yellow center and the other end pointing outward. Squeeze bag so that frosting fans slightly and move tube outward about ¾ inch toward edge of nail. Stop pressure, lift tube away. The petals are formed from the center outward. Repeat procedure around nail, making a total of ten to twelve petals in all. Buttercream daisies may be piped directly onto a frosted cake.

### BACHELOR BUTTONS

*Fit two decorating bags with couplings. Fill one bag with medium-blue icing (tint with royal or navy-blue paste color and a bit of violet). Set aside tube 13 to be attached later. Fill the other bag with dark blue icing and attach tube 3. Cut a sheet of waxed paper into 2-inch squares.*

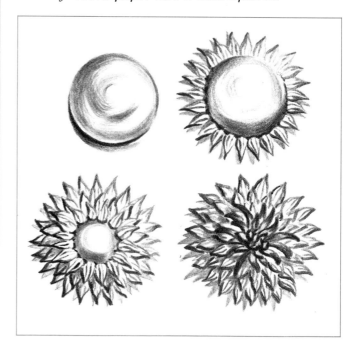

**1.** Attach a paper square to a flower nail with a dab of icing. Using the medium blue icing and the open coupling, squeeze a button base about 1 inch in diameter in the center of the nail. If pointed, tap it flat with a dampened finger; the base should resemble a flattened mound.

**2.** Attach tube 13 to the bag of medium blue icing. Hold bag almost parallel to the nail's surface with the tube touching any point at the base of the center button. Squeeze bag, pulling out slightly to form a spiked petal, then stop pressure and pull tube away. Repeat procedure to completely surround the base. Make another row of petals on top of the first, then finally make a third row.

**3.** Hold bag of dark blue icing perpendicular to the top of the flower and fill in the crown of the button with tube 3 points, pulling them out about ¼ inch.

### A WORD ABOUT ROSES

More frosting goes into making a rose than any other flower. Because they are so bulky, it's important to try to make them appear delicate. Piping roses with a very stiff icing, for example, will cause the edges of the petals to break slightly, making them look more natural and fragile. Color, too, plays an important role. A two-tone rose, for example, looks more beautiful and alive than one made with a solid shade. Try some of the following color hints when making your roses:

▪ Using a small spatula, fill one side of the decorating bag with a lighter color, the other side with a deeper shade of contrasting color, such as pink and yellow. Align wide end of tube with the side of the bag containing the darker shade.

▪ Using an artist's brush, paint a smeared line, about ⅛ to ¼ inch wide, with diluted food color along the seam of the decorating bag from the very bottom about two-thirds of the way up. The food colors, liquid or paste, should be diluted with a small amount of vodka, light rum or kirsch. Fill bag with icing; align narrow end of tube with the painted stripe.

▪ Use two decorating bags: one filled with a light color, the other with a deeper shade. You will also need two tubes to attach to the bags; they can be the same size or different by one number, 103 and 104, for example. Pipe the base and center of the rose with the deeper shade; pipe the other petals with the lighter shade.

Step 1

Step 2

Step 3

Step 4

Step 5

■ To add just a touch of contrasting color, dilute liquid or paste food color with vodka, light rum or kirsch and gently paint edges of petals with a small brush.

### THE PERFECT ROSE

*Fit a decorating bag with a coupling and fill bag with stiffened buttercream or royal icing, the color of your choice. Cut a sheet of waxed paper into 3-inch squares.*

1. Using a dab of frosting as glue, attach a waxed-paper square to a flower nail. To form a base for the rose, use the hole of the coupling (without a metal tube) to pipe a large dome-shaped mound onto the center of waxed paper. (See drawings, page 43.)

2. Attach rose tube 103 or 104 to the coupling. Hold bag with the narrow end of the tube pointing upward and the wide end touching just below the top of the domed base. To form a central bud, squeeze frosting and simultaneously turn the nail with your other hand. Make a continuous upright band, overlapping itself once or twice around the top of the dome. Stop pressure, lift tube away.

3. Hold bag with the narrow end of the tube pointing upward and the wide end touching any point at the base of the central bud. To form the first petal, squeeze bag, moving it slightly up and then down again as you simultaneously twist the nail with your other hand. Stop pressure, lift tube away. Repeat procedure to make two more petals so that the central bud is surrounded by three petals in all.

4. Continue making petals until the rose is as large as you would like it to be. Always begin each new petal at the middle base of the previous petal so that they will overlap. For a full-bloom effect, tilt the narrow end of the tube slightly outward when you make the final row of petals.

5. Immediately after piping, dust your fingers with cornstarch or confectioners' sugar and curl edges of a few petals under.

Carefully place the waxed paper with the rose on a tray. Air-dry roses made from royal icing overnight; air-dry buttercream roses for several hours, then freeze until needed or refrigerate for up to a week. Thaw frozen roses overnight in the refrigerator. Use a small spatula to transfer buttercream rose from paper to cake, or slip the tips of a partially opened pair of kitchen scissors beneath the rose and lift it off the paper. Position rose on cake, close and remove scissors.

**Note:** If you are going to pipe a lot of roses, it is easier to work with two decorating bags, fitted with couplings, so that you don't have to keep removing and attaching the rose tube with each new flower. Use one bag with open coupling to form the rose bases. The other with rose tube attached to form the petals.

### ROSEBUDS

Follow steps 1, 2 and 3 for making roses. Holding the flower nail in one hand, gently snap your wrist so that the rose falls slightly to one side. If it won't budge, push it over with a toothpick. Pipe two or three more petals around the sides and top of the toppled flower. Remove excess frosting from the central base with the edge of a toothpick.

# My Favorite Recipes

# Time-tested Cakes

It is quite true that one can produce a very tasty, light and moist cake with minimal effort in the kitchen by using a packaged cake mix. I especially like the flavor and texture of those which require the addition of butter, and I usually keep a box or two of mix on hand for those short-notice occasions when I don't have time to bake a cake from scratch. However, as good as some packaged mixes can be, they still can't match that special appeal and uniqueness of honest-to-goodness homemade cake. If you are going to take the time and trouble to decorate a special cake, then the cake itself should be just as good as you can possibly make it.

I have collected hundreds of recipes over the years, some better than others. Those included in this chapter are my favorites for cakes, frostings and decorations. I hope that you enjoy them as much as my family and friends.

Use the following table as a guideline when baking Auntie Alice's Golden Cake, Feather White Cake, Chocolate Fudge Cake, Double Chocolate Cake or White Chocolate Cake. It's possible that a cake may take longer to bake than the time specified, so be sure to check the cake with a cake tester (metal

| BAKING CHART | |
|---|---|
| SIZE | APPROXIMATE TIME |
| Three 8″ × 1½″ round layers | 25-30 minutes |
| Two 9″ × 1½″ or 2″ round layers | 30-35 minutes |
| Two 6″ × 6″ × 3″ square layers | 35-40 minutes |
| Two 8″ × 8″ × 2″ square layers | 30-35 minutes |
| One 9″ × 9″ × 2″ square layer | 45-50 minutes |
| One 9″ × 13″ × 2″ oblong layer | 40-45 minutes |
| One 11″ × 17″ × 1″ oblong layer | 20-25 minutes |
| One 10″ tube cake | 45-50 minutes |
| Thirty cup cakes | 15-20 minutes |

skewer, knife blade, toothpick or broom straw) before removing it from the oven. If the tester comes out clean when you insert it in the center of the cake, the cake is done. If particles cling to the tester, the cake will require additional baking. Test oblong cakes in several places to determine their readiness.

## Feather white cake

This cake has a moist, velvety crumb texture. A delicate hint of almond adds interest to its flavor and compensates for that which is lost by the omission of egg yolks in the recipe due to their coloring.

¾ cup (1½ sticks) unsalted butter, softened

¼ cup white vegetable shortening

2 cups granulated sugar

2 teaspoons vanilla extract

½ teaspoon almond extract

4 cups sifted cake flour

5 teaspoons baking powder

1¼ teaspoons salt

1⅓ cups milk, at cool-room temperature

7 egg whites, at room temperature

**1.** Preheat oven to 350 degrees. Grease cake pan(s), line the bottom with parchment paper and grease the paper. Flour the lined pan(s).

2. Cream the butter and shortening together in a large mixing bowl. Gradually add the sugar, beating until light and fluffy. Beat in the vanilla and almond extracts.

3. Combine the flour, baking powder and salt; stir gently to mix. With the mixer set at lowest speed, add it to the butter mixture alternately with the milk, beating only long enough to blend. Stop mixer; scrape down sides of bowl; beat at medium speed for 1 minute. (Do not overmix.)

4. Beat the egg whites only until they form soft peaks. Fold them into the batter.

5. Turn batter into the prepared pan(s) and bake according to the time table until a cake tester inserted in the center of the cake comes out clean.

6. Cool in the pan(s) on a rack for 10 minutes, then loosen the sides with a spatula or knife and turn out. Carefully peel off parchment. Finish cooling on rack.

## Chocolate fudge cake

Preparing a chocolate custard and then combining it with the remaining batter ingredients is the secret behind the moist, dark, fudgy character of this cake, a chocolate-lover's delight.

*5 eggs*
*2¼ cups granulated sugar*
*5 ounces unsweetened chocolate*
*1¾ cups milk*
*¾ cup (1½ sticks) butter, softened*
*2 teaspoons vanilla extract*
*2 teaspoons baking soda*
*1 teaspoon salt*
*3 cups sifted cake flour*

1. Preheat oven to 350 degrees. Grease cake pan(s), line the bottom(s) with parchment paper and grease the paper. Flour the lined pan(s).

2. Combine 1 egg, 1 cup sugar, the chocolate and ¾ cup milk in a saucepan. Cook, stirring, over low heat, until the chocolate melts and the mixture thickens slightly. Do not allow it to boil. Set aside to cool.

3. Cream butter with the remaining sugar until light and fluffy. Add the vanilla. Add the remaining eggs one at a time, beating well after each.

4. Stir the baking soda, salt and flour together and add it to the butter mixture alternately with the cup of remaining milk, beating only long enough to blend. Blend in the chocolate mixture.

5. Turn batter into the prepared pan(s) and bake according to the time table or until a cake tester inserted in the center of the cake comes out clean. (Do not overbake or cake will be dry.)

6. Cool in the pan(s) on a rack for 10 minutes, then loosen the sides with a spatula or knife and turn out. Carefully peel off parchment. Finish cooling on the rack.

## White chocolate cake

The color of this unusual cake is ivory, but the flavor is reminiscent of chocolate. It is made with white chocolate, which is sold in irregular chunks at confectionary stores or through mail-order suppliers.

*4 ounces white chocolate, broken into small pieces*
*⅓ cup boiling water*
*1 cup (2 sticks) butter, softened*
*2 cups granulated sugar*
*1 teaspoon vanilla extract*
*4 eggs, separated*
*2½ cups sifted cake flour*
*1 teaspoon baking soda*
*¼ teaspoon salt*
*1 cup buttermilk, at cool-room temperature*

1. Preheat oven to 350 degrees. Grease cake pan(s), line bottom(s) with parchment paper and grease the paper. Flour the lined pan(s).

2. Melt white chocolate in the boiling water, stirring occasionally. Set aside to cool.

3. Cream the butter in a large mixing bowl. Gradually add the sugar, beating until light and fluffy. Add the vanilla extract, then gradually beat in the egg yolks. Beat in the melted chocolate.

4. Stir the flour, baking soda and salt together. With the mixer set at lowest speed, add it to the butter mixture alternately with the buttermilk, beating only long enough to blend. Stop mixer; scrape down sides of bowl, then beat at medium speed for 1 minute. (Do not overbeat.)

5. Beat the egg whites only until they form soft peaks.

Fold them into the batter. Turn batter into the prepared pan(s) and bake according to the timetable, until a cake tester inserted in the center of the cake comes out clean.

**6.** Cool in the pan(s) on a rack for 10 minutes, then loosen the sides with a spatula or knife and turn out. Carefully peel off parchment. Finish cooling on the rack.

## Auntie Alice's golden cake

This is my all-time favorite cake recipe, and I never tire of it. After it has been in the oven for about 20 minutes, it fills the house with a delicious, lingering aroma that conjures up childhood memories of my Auntie Alice's kitchen. Egg yolks and butter lend incomparable flavor to this very tender, golden-colored cake.

*1 cup (2 sticks) butter, softened*
*2 cups granulated sugar*
*2½ teaspoons vanilla extract*
*8 egg yolks or 4 eggs, separated*
*4 cups sifted cake flour*
*5 teaspoons baking powder*
*1¼ teaspoons salt*
*1⅓ cups milk, at cool-room temperature*

**1.** Preheat oven to 350 degrees. Grease cake pan(s), line bottom(s) with parchment paper and grease the paper. Flour the lined pan(s).
**2.** Cream the butter in a large mixing bowl. Gradually add the sugar, beating until light and fluffy. Add the vanilla extract, then gradually beat in the egg yolks. (If using whole eggs, add the yolks one at a time, beating well after each addition. Set the egg whites aside.)
**3.** Stir the flour, baking powder and salt together. With the mixer set at lowest speed, add the dry mixture to the butter mixture alternately with the milk, beating only long enough to blend. Stop mixer; scrape down sides of bowl, then beat at medium speed for 1 minute. (Do not overbeat.)
**4.** Beat the egg whites only until they form soft peaks. Fold them into the batter.
**5.** Turn batter into the prepared pan(s) and bake according to the time table, until a cake tester inserted in the center of the cake comes out clean.

**6.** Cool in the pan(s) on a rack for 10 minutes, then loosen the sides with a spatula or knife and turn out. Carefully peel off parchment. Finish cooling on the rack.

## Double chocolate cake

This has got to be the best chocolate cake ever. It's moist and absolutely sensational. Because it sinks slightly upon cooling, it requires little, if any, leveling.

*2 ounces semisweet chocolate, broken up*
*2 ounces sweet chocolate, broken up*
*½ cup boiling water*
*1 cup (2 sticks) butter, softened*
*2 cups granulated sugar*
*1½ teaspoons vanilla extract*
*4 eggs, separated*
*2½ cups sifted cake flour*
*1 teaspoon baking soda*
*½ teaspoon salt*
*½ cup buttermilk, at cool room temperature*

**1.** Preheat oven to 350 degrees. Grease cake pan(s), line bottom(s) with parchment paper and grease the paper. Flour the lined pan(s).
**2.** Melt chocolate in the boiling water, stirring occasionally. Set aside to cool.
**3.** Cream the butter in a large mixing bowl. Gradually add the sugar, beating until light and fluffy. Add the vanilla extract, then gradually beat in the egg yolks. Beat in the melted chocolate.
**4.** Stir the cake flour, baking soda and salt together. With the mixer set at lowest speed, add it to the butter mixture alternately with the buttermilk, beating only long enough to blend. Stop mixer; scrape down sides of bowl, then beat at medium speed for 1 minute. (Do not overbeat.)
**5.** Beat the egg whites only until they form soft peaks. Fold them into the batter. Turn batter into the prepared pan(s) and bake according to the timetable, until a cake tester inserted in the center of the cake comes out clean. Don't overbake, or cake will be dry.
**6.** Cool in the pan(s) on a rack for 10 minutes, then loosen the sides with a spatula or knife and turn out. Carefully peel off the parchment. Finish cooling on the rack.

## Three-tier gold or silver cake

This is a recipe for a pale golden cake which will serve up to 88 people if cut as suggested on page 27. To make a white cake, use the specified amount of egg whites instead of whole eggs. The cake tiers—6, 9 and 12 inches in diameter, each about 3 inches high—are formed from two layers, rather than a single thick layer. Thus, six pans are necessary, and each should be filled equally with about 1 inch of batter, regardless of how deep the pans might be. When baked, each layer will be approximately 1½ inches high, so that when leveled and assembled with frosting, each tier will be about 3 inches high.

Because of the quantity of batter involved, it's easier to prepare and bake the 6- and 9-inch layers separately from the 12-inch layers. Depending on the size of your oven, you may be able to bake only two layers at a time. In this case, the remaining batter should be poured into the appropriate prepared pans and refrigerated until they are able to be placed in the oven. An electric mixer with a 4½- to 5-quart bowl is an absolute must; don't use a hand mixer.

**BATTER FOR 6- AND 9-INCH LAYERS:**
*1 cup (2 sticks) butter, softened*
*½ cup white vegetable shortening*
*3 cups granulated sugar*
*5 eggs, separated (or 10 egg whites)*
*6 cups sifted cake flour*
*2 tablespoons baking powder*
*1 teaspoon salt*
*2 cups milk, at cool-room temperature*
*1 tablespoon vanilla extract*
*1 teaspoon almond extract*

**BATTER FOR 12-INCH LAYERS:**
*1½ cups (3 sticks) butter, softened*
*½ cup white vegetable shortening*
*7 eggs, separated (or 14 egg whites)*
*4 cups granulated sugar*
*8 cups sifted cake flour*
*2 tablespoons, plus 2 teaspoons baking powder*
*1½ teaspoons salt*
*2⅔ cups milk, at cool-room temperature*
*4 teaspoons vanilla extract*
*1¼ teaspoons almond extract*

**1.** Prepare two 6- by 2-inch, two 9- by 2-inch and two 12- by 2-inch round cake pans. Grease sides and bottoms with shortening, then line bottoms with parchment and grease the top of each paper. Flour each greased and lined pan; invert and tap pan lightly to remove excess flour. Preheat oven to 350 degrees.

**2.** For 6- by 9-inch layers: Cream the butter and shortening until smooth. Slowly and gradually add the sugar, beating until light and fluffy. If using whole eggs, add yolks one at a time, beating well after each addition. Set egg whites aside.

**3.** Combine flour, baking powder and salt in a large bowl, stirring until well mixed. With the mixer set at lowest speed, add it to the butter mixture alternately with the milk, beating only long enough to blend. Stop mixer; scrape sides of bowl, then beat at medium speed for 1 minute. Do not overbeat.

**4.** Beat egg whites only until they form soft peaks. Fold them into the batter. Turn batter into the prepared pans, filling each to the same level. (Use a ruler to accurately measure the height of the batter.) Bake 6-inch layers for about 35 minutes, 9-inch layers for about 45 minutes. Cakes are done when a cake tester inserted in the center comes out clean. Do not overbake or wait until cakes pull away from the sides of the pans to remove from oven.

**5.** Cool cakes in pans for 10 minutes before turning out onto racks to cool completely. Carefully peel off parchment.

**6.** For 12-inch layers: Follow above instructions using quantities of ingredients listed above for 12-inch layers. Bake 12-inch layers for 45 to 55 minutes. Cool in pans for 20 minutes before turning out onto racks to cool completely.

## Vanilla brandy-yogurt cake

Here's a tender, moist and delicious cake that is baked in a tube pan.

*1 cup (2 sticks) butter, softened*
*2 cups granulated sugar*
*6 eggs, separated*
*1 teaspoon vanilla extract*
*3 cups sifted cake flour*
*1 teaspoon baking soda*
*¼ teaspoon salt*
*1 cup plain yogurt*
*2 tablespoons brandy*

1. Preheat oven to 350 degrees. Grease and flour a 10-inch tube pan.

2. In a large mixing bowl, beat butter with 1½ cups sugar until creamy. Add egg yolks and vanilla, beating until thick, about 5 minutes.

3. Combine the flour, baking soda and salt. Alternately mix the flour and yogurt into the creamed butter mixture. Stir in the brandy. Beat egg whites until they form soft peaks; then gradually add the remaining ½ cup sugar, beating until glossy. Fold egg whites into batter.

4. Turn mixture into the prepared pan. Bake for 45 minutes, or until a cake tester inserted in the center comes out clean. Cool 15 minutes in pan, then turn out onto a rack. Cool completely.

## Chocolate cake roll

This is not a true sponge cake, for it contains baking powder and butter. It may be filled with a variety of fillings, including jelly, fruit or cream, but the chocolate flavor goes exceedingly well with Classic Buttercream.

*1½ cups sifted cake flour*

*7 tablespoons unsweetened cocoa*

*1½ teaspoons baking powder*

*⅜ teaspoon salt*

*5 eggs*

*1¼ cups granulated sugar*

*1 teaspoon vanilla extract*

*½ teaspoon rum extract*

*½ cup water*

*2 tablespoons melted butter*

*Confectioners' sugar*

1. Preheat oven to 375 degrees. Line a 17- by 11- by 1-inch jelly-roll pan with parchment paper.

2. Combine the flour, cocoa, baking powder, and salt; stir to mix.

3. In a medium-sized mixing bowl, beat the eggs on high speed for about 5 minutes, or until very thick. Gradually beat in the granulated sugar until mixture makes a ribbon trail when beaters are lifted. On low speed, blend in the vanilla, rum extract, and water. Add the flour mixture all at once, beating just until smooth. Quickly beat in melted butter.

4. Pour batter into the prepared pan, spreading it evenly and well into the corners. Bake for 14 to 16 minutes, or until cake feels firm in the center. Do not overbake or it will crack when rolled.

5. Immediately loosen the edges of the cake with a knife and turn out onto a clean, flat-weave dish towel sprinkled with confectioners' sugar. Carefully peel off the paper lining. Trim off the stiff edges, removing about ¼ inch with a sharp knife. Starting at the narrow end, roll warm cake together with the towel, jelly-roll fashion. (The towel will be inside the cake.) Place seam-side down and cool thoroughly on a wire rack. When ready to decorate, unroll cake, spread with desired filling such as Classic Buttercream, then reroll.

## White velvet fruitcake

Few fruitcakes, in my opinion, combine well with buttercream frosting. This cake, rich but delicately flavored, is an exception.

*1 pound pecan halves, coarsely chopped*

*½ pound candied cherries, halved*

*½ pound mixed candied fruits*

*½ pound golden raisins*

*4 cups sifted all-purpose flour*

*1½ cups (3 sticks) butter, softened*

*2 cups granulated sugar*

*6 eggs, separated*

*¾ cup half-and-half*

*¼ cup applesauce*

*1 teaspoon almond extract*

*½ teaspoon vanilla extract*

*1 teaspoon cream of tartar*

*2 tablespoons brandy, rum or bourbon (optional)*

1. Preheat oven to 275 degrees. Grease a 10-inch tube pan. Line the bottom of the pan with parchment paper and grease the paper.

2. In a very large bowl or pan (about 8 quarts), combine the nuts, cherries, fruits, raisins and ½ cup of flour. Use a large spoon to stir the mixture thoroughly. Set aside.

3. In a large mixing bowl, cream the butter until smooth, adding the sugar gradually. Add the egg yolks, one at a time, and beat with an electric mixer until smooth and light, about 4 minutes.

4. Combine the half-and-half, applesauce, almond and vanilla extracts. Beat into the creamed mixture alternately with the remaining flour. (This cake needs

no baking powder.) Stop beating as soon as everything is blended together. Pour batter over the fruit and nut mixture and stir to mix.

**5.** In another bowl, beat the egg whites until foamy, then add cream of tartar. Continue beating until stiff, but not dry. Fold into the fruit and nut batter.

**6.** Ladle the batter into the prepared pan and press it down with the back of a spoon. Bake for 3¼ hours, or until a cake tester inserted in the center comes out clean.

**7.** Remove from oven and sprinkle two tablespoons of brandy over the cake. Cool cake in pan for 30 minutes, then turn out onto a wire rack to cool completely. Peel off paper and wrap cake tightly in plastic wrap. Cover with foil; store in a cool place until ready to frost and decorate.

*Note:* This recipe may also be baked in two 5- by 9- by 3-inch loaf pans for 2¼ hours or in two 6- by 6- by 3-inch square pans for 2¼ hours.

## Scrap cake

Here's a great idea for using up leftover pieces of cake. Simply cut them into ¾-inch cubes and fold them into this feather-light chocolate mousse. Unmold the dessert and decorate it any way you like using the recipe for Stabilized Decorating Cream (page 56).

*1 tablespoon unflavored gelatin*
*¼ cup cold water*
*8 egg yolks*
*¾ cup granulated sugar*
*1½ cups milk, scalded*
*6 ounces semisweet chocolate, melted*
*1½ cups heavy cream, whipped*
*3 cups freshly cut cake cubes*

**1.** Lightly oil an 8-cup cake pan, bowl or gelatin mold. Sprinkle the gelatin over the water and let stand to soften.

**2.** Beat the egg yolks in a medium-sized saucepan until thick and creamy, about 5 minutes. Gradually beat in the sugar. Slowly add the scalded milk, beating constantly. Cook, stirring, over low heat until mixture coats a spoon. Do not boil. Remove from heat; stir in gelatin and melted chocolate.

**3.** Cool to room temperature, stirring occasionally. Fold in the whipped cream; fold in the cake cubes. Turn mixture into the prepared pan, cover with plastic wrap and chill until set, about 5 hours or overnight.

**4.** To unmold, run a knife around the edge of the mold to loosen the mousse. Tilt the mold with one hand and with the other insert the knife (at any point along the edge) down to the bottom of the mold while gently pulling the gelatin away from the side of the mold. This will break the air lock. Remove the knife. Place your serving dish over the top of the mold and, holding both firmly together, turn them over (right side up). Gently give the mold a sideways shake or two and the mousse should slip out.

**5.** Decorate with Stabilized Decorating Cream; chill, covered, until ready to serve.

# Fabulous Frostings and Decorations

## Buttercreams

Although there are many different kinds of cake frostings and fillings, few are as delicious and multipurpose as Classic Buttercream. It makes a tasty filling, covers cakes smoothly and pipes well-defined borders and other decorations. The surface of the frosting crystallizes and dries to a crisp coat while the inner portion remains feathery light and creamy.

The recipe below needs no cooking. Buttercream tints well and stays fresh for at least two weeks if kept tightly covered in the refrigerator. To use stored frosting, allow it to come to cool-room temperature and then beat again for a few minutes to restore its fluffy consistency.

To thin a small amount of buttercream for printing, writing or piping drop strings, simply beat in milk or water by drops until the buttercream can easily flow from the tube when gentle pressure is applied to the decorating bag.

To stiffen buttercream for piping flowers on a flower nail or directly onto a frosted cake, beat in additional sifted confectioners' sugar by spoonfuls until the buttercream is firm enough to hold the curve of a petal.

Buttercream flowers that have been piped on a nail should be air-dried and placed in the refrigerator to thoroughly chill before attempting to remove them from their waxed-paper base.

I always try to make a few extra flowers in case of breakage and keep some extra frosting for touching up minor flaws that might occur when the flowers are transferred onto the cake.

The following recipe may be halved or doubled, if desired. A heavy-duty mixer is recommended for the extensive beating.

### Classic buttercream

*¾ cup (1½ sticks) unsalted butter, at room temperature*
*¼ cup white vegetable shortening*
*½ cup milk*
*¼ teaspoon salt*
*1½ teaspoons vanilla extract*
*2 pounds confectioners' sugar, sifted.*

Place butter, shortening, milk, salt, vanilla extract and one pound of sugar in a large mixing bowl. Beat at low speed until combined, then gradually add the remaining pound of sugar. Stop mixer and scrape the sides of the bowl. Resume beating on high speed until mixture is light and fluffy, about 8 to 10 minutes. Keep buttercream covered with plastic wrap to prevent crusting while you work on the cake. If your kitchen is very warm, the frosting may become too soft to hold its shape; place it in the refrigerator until it firms up enough for work to continue.

*Yield:* about 5 cups.

### Chocolate buttercream

**1.** Make Classic Buttercream according to directions. You may divide the buttercream in half, make the entire batch chocolate, or even double the recipe. For each pound of sugar used in preparing the buttercream, allow ⅔ cup sifted unsweetened cocoa, 3 tablespoons softened butter and ⅛ teaspoon salt.
**2.** Add the cocoa, butter and salt to the Classic Buttercream and beat until thoroughly distributed.

**3.** Add milk by teaspoonfuls until frosting is the desired consistency—stiff, medium or thin. If a deeper shade is desired, add a bit of brown food coloring.

## Mocha buttercream

Make chocolate buttercream, but replace the final teaspoons of milk with an equal amount of strong black coffee.

## Bette's decoration buttercream

The appearance of this buttercream is very similar to Classic Buttercream, but it behaves differently because there isn't any butter in the recipe. Decoration buttercream is stiffer, the perfect consistency for making roses; it doesn't weep or soften as quickly; it dries slightly crisper; its flavor harmonizes with the classic version so that when decorations made from it are used on a cake frosted with classic, the difference is hardly noticeable.

This frosting is ideal for those times when you want to make a large batch of roses or other sturdy flowers in advance. Simply place the waxed-paper squares containing the freshly made flowers on a tray;

air-dry for at least an hour, until slightly crisp; cover the tray with foil, then refrigerate to harden. Do not attempt to remove flowers from their waxed-paper squares until completely chilled. The longer they remain in the refrigerator, the firmer they become. They keep nicely for about two weeks. If you want to keep them longer, they may be frozen and then thawed in the refrigerator overnight.

*1¼ cups white vegetable shortening*
*1 pound confectioners' sugar, sifted*
*3 tablespoons water*
*1 teaspoon vanilla extract*
*¼ teaspoon salt*

**1.** Place all ingredients into a large mixing bowl. Beat at low speed until combined.
**2.** Stop mixer and scrape the sides of the bowl. Resume beating on high speed until mixture is light and fluffy, about 5 minutes.
**3.** Keep bowl covered with plastic wrap to prevent crusting while you work.

*Yield:* about 2 cups.

# Royal icings

The most important thing to remember about this ornamental icing is that it hardens as it dries, so that decorations made from it are firm and easy to handle. Because it is so strong, it is often used to decorate dummy display cakes that will last for months. On the other hand, royal icing isn't as palatable as buttercream and shouldn't be used for frosting a real cake. It is the best choice for making fragile flowers and other small, intricate decorations that are too difficult to pipe directly onto a cake.

Royal-icing decorations must be made in advance and allowed time to air-dry completely, usually overnight. The decorations can then be stored in a sealed container at room temperature until needed, weeks or months later.

There are two ways to make royal icing. One recipe calls for the use of fresh egg whites, which produces a very fine quality icing. However, this icing must be used immediately, because it softens and begins to deteriorate in texture very quickly. Rebeating will not restore its texture. The recipe I

prefer to use calls for the use of meringue powder, which is usually sold by suppliers of cake decorating equipment. This icing can be stored in an airtight container in the refrigerator for up to two weeks and then beaten again by hand when ready to use.

Whichever recipe you decide to use, you will find that royal icing has a wonderfully pliable consistency and is easy to work with. Because both recipes must initially be beaten for 7 to 10 minutes, a heavy-duty mixer is recommended for their preparation. Stiffen icing by beating in additional confectioners' sugar; thin icing by whisking in teaspoons of lemon juice. When working with royal icing, keep bowl and tube ends covered with a damp paper towel or cloth. Pipe flowers onto waxed paper that has been attached to a flower nail with a dab of icing. Other decorations and simple flowers can be piped directly onto a sheet of waxed paper placed over a cookie sheet or cutting board for support. Air-dry the decorations overnight, peel off the waxed paper and store at room temperature in a sealed container.

## Royal icing with meringue powder

*¼ cup meringue powder*
*½ cup cold water*
*1 pound confectioners' sugar, sifted*

**1.** Be sure utensils are squeaky clean and free of grease.
**2.** Combine meringue powder and water in a large mixing bowl, beat until mixture forms soft peaks.
**3.** Add sugar and continue beating until fluffy and voluminous, about 7 minutes. Icing should be able to peak to an inch or more.
**4.** For softer icing, add up to 1 tablespoon of water, beating in by teaspoons, to the desired decoration consistency. Tint as desired.

*Yield:* about 3 cups

## Royal icing with egg whites

*1 pound confectioners sugar, sifted*
*3 large egg whites, at room temperature (see note)*
*½ teaspoon cream of tartar*
*¼ teaspoon vanilla extract*

**1.** Be sure utensils are squeaky clean and free of grease.
**2.** Place all ingredients in a large bowl and beat at low speed until combined. Stop power and scrape down sides of bowl with a rubber spatula.
**3.** Turn to high speed and beat until fluffy and voluminous, about 7 minutes. Tint icing as desired and use immediately.

*Yield:* about 2½ cups
   *Note:* Do not use extra large eggs.

# More frostings and glazes

## Quick fondant icing

This is a runny icing used only for covering cakes and petit fours. Its consistency should be thin enough to be poured, but thick enough to cling to the cake. Fondant sets quickly and provides a smooth, glossy background that enhances buttercream decorations piped over it. (See Loving Heart on page 164.) In addition, a smooth, thin layer of buttercream spread over the cake before pouring on the fondant helps ensure a flawless finish. The buttercream layer may be omitted, if desired, provided the cake has been spread with jam glaze. But, in this case, you may need to apply a second coat of fondant to ensure complete coverage.

*½ cup warm water*
*½ cup light corn syrup*
*2 pounds confectioners' sugar*
*½ teaspoon vanilla extract*
*2 teaspoons raw egg white*
*1 tablespoon melted butter*

**1.** Place water, corn syrup and sugar in top of double boiler; stir with a wood spoon until well mixed.
**2.** Heat over hot water just until lukewarm. Do not let the temperature of the fondant rise above 100 degrees or it will lose its gloss. If necessary, thin fondant with a little more warm water or thicken it with additional confectioners' sugar.
**3.** Gently stir in vanilla extract, egg white and butter, being careful to avoid air bubbles.
**4.** Tint with food color, if desired. Bang pan several times on a wood board or other hard surface to remove as many air bubbles as possible before pouring.
**5.** To cover cake, first spread with a layer of jam glaze and allow to set for about an hour. Then, if desired spread a smooth, thin layer of buttercream over top and sides and allow to set for 20 minutes.
**6.** Place cake on a rack with a cookie sheet or waxed paper underneath to catch drips. Pour fondant over top of cake working from the center outward and using a spatula to guide it evenly. Puncture air bubbles with a straight pin as soon as they appear.
**7.** Allow about 15 minutes for the fondant to set, then trim the bottom edges of the cake with a sharp knife. Fondant that drips onto the cookie sheet may be scraped up, reheated and used again. If necessary, thin with a little warm water.

*Yield:* about 5 cups.

## Quick chocolate fondant icing

Add one or more ounces of melted semisweet chocolate to prepared Quick Fondant Icing, depending on the color and flavor intensity desired.

## Rich chocolate glaze

If ever there was a contest for versatile recipes, this one would be a top contender. It is wonderful as a filling or icing for cakes and cookies, but it can also be used as a topping for ice cream, éclairs, and cream puffs. In addition, it makes a delicious fondue with fresh fruit dippers. The recipe can be proportionately decreased or increased, if desired.

*12 ounces sweet chocolate*

*2 tablespoons butter*

*6 tablespoons light corn syrup*

*¼ cup milk*

*¼ teaspoon rum, orange or vanilla extract*

Melt the chocolate and butter in the top of a double boiler over hot water. Add the corn syrup and milk, stirring until mixed. Stir in the extract. Use while hot.

## Jam glaze

Traditionally, a jam glaze should be made with apricot preserves, and I must admit that they are my favorite. However, other flavors can work equally well. A marmalade or raspberry glaze over chocolate cake, for example, makes a nice change when you are in the mood for something different. Be wary about choosing a red glaze over cake to be frosted with white icing as the color may cast a tint.

*12 ounce jar jam or jelly*

*1 tablespoon lemon juice*

*2 tablespoons water*

1. Place all ingredients into a saucepan and heat until boiling.

2. If using jam, strain through a medium-fine sieve to remove the pulp.

3. Place cake on a rack over a cookie sheet or sheet of waxed paper. Brush warm liquid over cake. Reheat, if necessary.

4. Before frosting, air-dry cake for about an hour until glaze is set. Leftover glaze may be stored in the refrigerator or added back to the pulp and used in the normal manner.

*Yield:* About 1 cup.

## Stabilized decorating cream

This is a recipe for homemade whipped cream that can be used in a decorating bag. Although I haven't used it on any of the cakes pictured in this book, it is included here because it is ideal for decorating the Scrap Cake which is also found in this section. This cream is very light, but it can still produce much the same decorating results as buttercream, with sharp and clear designs. Any leftover Decorating Cream can be piped into rosettes, stars, flowers and so forth on a cookie sheet and then frozen. The decorations can then be transferred to a plastic bag and stored in a freezer for weeks. Simply place the frozen decorations on any dessert. They are easy to handle when hard and take only a few minutes to soften once in place.

*Note:* Do not attempt to use whipped cream that has not been stabilized in a decorating bag. The warmth of your hand and the squeezing will cause the untreated cream to separate, producing soft, mushy designs.

*2 teaspoons water*

*3 teaspoons brandy, rum or any liqueur*

*1 teaspoon unflavored gelatin*

*1 cup heavy whipping cream, cold*

*¼ cup confectioners' sugar*

1. Chill all utensils in the refrigerator (bowl, beaters, decorating bag and tubes). Also chill the cake that is to be decorated.

2. In a small heat-resistant cup, sprinkle the gelatin over the water and brandy, and let stand for 5 minutes to soften. Place cup in a pan of very hot water, stirring until gelatin is dissolved. Remove from heat and gently stir until the dissolved gelatin reaches room temperature.

3. Beat the cream in the chilled bowl while the gelatin is cooling. (Remember to give the gelatin an occasional stir so that it doesn't solidify at the bottom of the cup.) When the cream is beaten to a medium

consistency, stop beating. Add the sugar and gelatin all at once. Resume beating until the cream stands in stiff peaks. (Do not overbeat.)

4. Wash your hands with cold water. Immediately place the cream in the chilled decorating bag and decorate your dessert. Do not chill the stabilized cream before use, but rather work as quickly as you can. The decorated dessert then may be placed in the refrigerator, where it will keep nicely for up to two days. Cover so that it doesn't absorb any other food odors.

*Yield:* about 2 cups.

## Dramatic decorations

### Shaved chocolate bark

When the weather is cool and dry, this recipe may be made with semisweet chocolate. On hot, damp or rainy days, however, it works better with dark chocolate summer coating.

*1 pound semisweet chocolate, or*
*1 pound dark chocolate summer coating*

1. Melt chocolate or summer coating in a pan over hot water, occasionally stirring with a wood spoon.
2. Pour the melted chocolate or summer coating onto a large marble slab, spreading it very thinly, about 1/16 inch thick. (If you don't have access to a marble slab, you can use a Formica-like surface, but the chocolate will take longer to cool.)
3. Let cool until almost dry, about 5 minutes. It shouldn't have a tacky feeling when touched lightly with the fingertips.
4. Holding a sugar scraper or a large chef's knife at an angle, push the blade under the edge of the chocolate and away from yourself with a short, quick motion. Repeat procedure to form rough curls and peels.
5. Transfer curls to a cookie sheet as you work, piling them in two or three layers. Chill in the refrigerator until hard, then transfer to a covered container. Store in the refrigerator until needed.

### Chocolate leaves

Chocolate leaves are surprisingly easy to make. Use semi-sweet chocolate when the weather is cool and dry. On hot, damp or rainy days work with dark chocolate summer coating.

*Several rose, lemon or geranium leaves*
*2 ounces semisweet chocolate or dark chocolate summer coating*

1. Gently wash the leaves and pat them dry between paper towels.
2. Melt chocolate or summer coating in a pan placed over hot water.
3. Using a small artist's brush, paint the veined *underside* of each leaf with a layer of melted chocolate, about 1/8 inch thick. Be careful not to let any chocolate run over onto the reverse side of the leaf.
4. Place leaves on a plate and chill in the refrigerator or freezer until chocolate hardens completely, about 10 minutes.
5. When ready to use, simply peel the leaf away from the chocolate starting at the stem end of the leaf. Handle the chocolate as little as possible. Discard natural leaves.

### Marzipan

If you have a food processor, preparing marzipan is a breeze. If not, a heavy-duty mixer can be used to lighten the initial task of manual mixing.

*2 medium egg whites*
*1/2 teaspoon vanilla extract*
*1 pound confectioners' sugar, sifted*
*8 ounces almond paste*

*Using food processor:* Combine all ingredients in work bowl fitted with a steel knife and mix until mixture forms a ball. If dough is too sticky, add a little more confectioners' sugar; if too stiff, add a few drops of light corn syrup.

*By hand:* Place egg whites, extract and sugar into a large mixing bowl. Beat at medium-low speed until combined. Add almond paste, a small amount at a time, beating until blended in. When dough becomes too stiff for mixer, add remaining almond paste and knead by hand. Continue kneading until dough is pliable and easy to handle, adding more sugar, if necessary, to stiffen it. Shape the dough into a ball.

*To color:* Use paste food colors to tint marzipan, kneading in a small amount of coloring at a time until the desired shade is achieved. Pastel colors taste best and are more attractive. For more intense color, finished decorations may be glazed with tinted corn syrup or painted with a small brush dipped into liquid food coloring that has been diluted with a small amount of kirsch, white rum or vodka.

For a rich brown color and a chocolate flavor, knead in unsweetened cocoa a little at a time. For a deep tan color and a coffee flavor, work in powdered instant coffee a little at a time. Soften with a few drops of light corn syrup if dough is too dry or stiff; knead in a little more sugar if too sticky.

*To shape:* Marzipan is very similar in texture to modeling clay, and making decorations from it is just as much fun as child's play. Keep the large ball of dough covered with plastic wrap as you work so that it doesn't dry out. Remove a small hunk and roll it into a ball between the palms of your hands. Shape it into any form you desire.

Or, sprinkle a sheet of plastic wrap with confectioners' sugar and place a flattened ball of marzipan in the center. Sprinkle with more sugar and cover with another piece of plastic wrap. Roll out just as you would pastry dough. Remove upper wrap, brush off excess sugar with a pastry brush, and run a spatula underneath the dough to make sure it hasn't stuck. Cut out decorative shapes freehand or with aspic or cookie cutters. The decorations may be used as is, sprinkled with colored sugar or glazed for a shiny appearance. Place all marzipan decorations on a tray lined with waxed paper to allow them to dry.

*To glaze:* Combine ¼ cup light corn syrup with 2 teaspoons hot water and stir until mixed. Tint, if desired, then using an artist's brush, paint surface of marzipan decorations.

*To store:* Cover the ball of marzipan with plastic wrap and place it in a sealed container in the refrigerator until needed. It will keep for at least a month. Marzipan may also be frozen for up to a year.

## Mock marzipan

If someone is allergic to nuts, or there is no almond paste on hand, or you are simply keeping a strict eye on your budget, the following recipe for mock marzipan may be used in place of the real thing. It handles just as easily and creates very tasty decorations. It is also useful whenever you need to make pure white decorations.

*2 large egg whites*
*2 tablespoons white vegetable shortening*
*1 tablespoon light corn syrup*
*1½ pounds (boxes) confectioners' sugar, sifted*
*1 teaspoon flavoring extract of your choice*

Place all ingredients into a large mixing bowl. Mix on slow speed of heavy-duty mixer until blended. Shape into a ball and cover with plastic wrap. Color, shape and store just as you would for marzipan.

## Crystallized flowers

Select edible flowers with simple, open petal arrangements such as black-eyed Susans, daisies, daylilies, forsythias, gladioli, hibiscus, honeysuckle, nasturtiums, orange blossoms, pansies and violets. Rose petals and mint leaves also work well. Superfine sugar is a must; do not use regular granulated or confectioners' sugar.

*Flowers*
*2 large egg whites, at room temperature*
*1 cup superfine sugar*

**1.** Line a large tray with waxed paper.
**2.** Remove pollinated parts of flowers, if necessary. Snip flowers leaving a small part of the stem to hold onto.
**3.** Lightly beat egg whites just enough to loosen them.
**4.** Holding a single flower by its stem, dip it into the egg white. Lift it out and use a small artist's brush to spread the egg white evenly but lightly, coating the entire flower and separating the petals.
**5.** Sprinkle lightly with sugar, covering all parts of the coated flower. Shake it gently to remove excess sugar. Set sugared flowers on the prepared tray and let air-dry several hours or overnight.

*Note:* Some crystallized flowers keep better than others. Those, such as gladioli, with fragile petals will fade in color after 24 hours.

# Cakes to Decorate

The following pages contain detailed instructions for
decorating thirty-six of the best cakes I have ever designed.
None is especially difficult to reproduce. If you can wield
a decorating bag—and a little practice is all it takes—you
will find each and every one of them fairly easy and
amusing to make in your own home.

# Special
# Party Cakes

# Rainbow Cake

Send someone off with a special wish for happiness. They may be taking a vacation, moving to a new home, starting college or a new job. Whenever you want to say, "Have a nice day," let this rainbow of happiness cake express your feelings and warm wishes. By the way, should you want to let someone know that you are unhappy and want to make up after an argument, simply pipe an inverted sunshine mouth. This cake is really quite easy to make, since most of it is decorated with a star tube and the clouds are swirled freehand with a spatula.

## Preparing the cake

*2 9-inch round cake layers, cooled to room temperature and leveled*

*1 recipe Jam Glaze*

*1 8-inch round cardboard base, covered with parchment*

**1.** Place cake layers on a rack; brush on warm jam glaze, then air-dry for about an hour to allow glaze to set.

**2.** Transfer one cake layer to the prepared cardboard base using a bit of glaze or buttercream to secure it in place. Spread a thin layer of white buttercream over the top, then position second layer on top of first.

**3.** Using a toothpick, mark top of cake by poking small holes to indicate a 2½-inch circle for the sun and about ¾-inch bands for the colors of the rainbow.

## Preparing the frosting

*1 recipe Classic Buttercream*

*Paste food colors: lavender, pink, orange, lemon yellow, sky blue, black*

Mix and tint buttercream the day before or while waiting for the glaze to set.

**1.** Place about ½ cup of buttercream into each of three small bowls; tint one bowl lavender, one bowl pink, and one bowl orange. Cover each with plastic wrap.

**2.** Place ¾ cup of buttercream into a small bowl and tint it yellow; cover with plastic wrap.

**3.** Divide remaining buttercream in half; tint one half blue and cover with plastic wrap; cover remaining white buttercream with plastic wrap.

## Decorating the cake

*Tubes: 4, 16*

*7 parchment cones*

**1.** Spread some yellow buttercream within the sun's circle, mounding it slightly higher in the center. Smooth the surface of the sun with a hot spatula. Set remaining yellow aside.

**2.** Spread some white buttercream below the sun and partly over his chin, swirling the spatula for a cloudlike effect.

**3.** Fit a parchment cone with tube 16 and fill with blue buttercream. Pipe stars around the side of the cake, starting at the lower edge and working up and over the top to form the outer band of the rainbow, about ¾-inch wide.

**4.** Discard the bag of blue buttercream; wash and dry tube 16. Fit a clean parchment cone with tube 16 and fill with lavender. Pipe a ¾-inch wide star band. Discard lavender and repeat process with pink and then orange.

**5.** Place remaining yellow buttercream in a parchment cone fitted with tube 4. Pipe rays of sun. Discard yellow; wash and dry tube 4.

**6.** Insert tube 4 into a clean parchment cone and fill with a small amount of white buttercream. Pipe two dots for the whites of the eyes. Discard white buttercream; wash and dry tube 4.

**7.** Combine a small amount of any color remaining buttercream in a bowl and tint black. Transfer to a fresh parchment cone fitted with tube 4. Pipe C's around the white of the eyes and finish with a happy sunshine smile.

# Haus-Segen Hex Cake

In eastern Pennsylvania, Dutch farmers paint their barns with colorful hex signs to bring them luck and good fortune and to *wilkom* (welcome) visitors. Inspired by this charming tradition, a cake decorated in the style of a Pennsylvania Dutch *haus-segen* (house blessing) hex sign makes an unusual gift to present to a new neighbor, a new home owner or a special friend who has recently moved into a new dwelling.

Although the work on top of the cake is intricate, the decorations are piped in buttercream, which dries to a crisp coat in a short period of time. If you goof, simply wait for the error to dry, then remove it with toothpicks and repipe the decoration. If you are wary about decorating the top of the cake in buttercream, you can, of course, pipe the birds, drop flowers and tulip-shaped petals in advance with royal icing.

## Preparing the cake

*2 9-inch round cake layers, cooled to room temperature and leveled*

*1 recipe Jam Glaze*

*9-inch round cardboard base, covered with parchment*

1. Place layers on a rack. Brush on warm jam glaze, then air-dry until set, about an hour.
2. Transfer one layer to prepared cardboard base, using a bit of jam glaze or buttercream to secure it in place.
3. Spread white buttercream over top of bottom layer, then position top layer in place.
4. Trace cake pattern onto parchment or tracing paper.

## Preparing the frosting

*1 recipe Classic Buttercream*

*Paste food colors: orange sherbet, yellow, super Christmas red, blue, green*

Mix and tint buttercream the day before or while waiting for glaze to set.

1. Place ¼ cup buttercream into each of four bowls. Tint red, green, orange and blue. Cover bowls with plastic wrap.
2. Divide remaining buttercream in half. Tint one bowl yellow, leave the other white. Cover bowls with plastic wrap.

## Decorating the cake

*Tubes: 1, 6, 13, 15, 17, 20, 32*

*5 decorating bags, fitted with couplings*

1. Frost top of cake with a smooth layer of white buttercream.
2. Place paper pattern on top of cake. Using a toothpick or metal skewer, puncture the pattern design onto the cake.
3. Fill a decorating bag with red buttercream; attach tube 1. Pipe dotted heart and message. Attach tube 15 to bag of red; pipe red portions of tulips.
4. Wash and dry tube 1. Attach to a decorating bag and fill with green. Pipe green stems and leaves.
5. Attach tube 32 to a decorating bag and fill with orange. Pipe a shell to form forward wing on birds. Attach tube 20 to bag of orange; pipe a shell to form rear wing on birds. Attach tube 13 to bag of orange, pipe drop flowers and orange portions of tulip. Attach tube 6 to bag of orange, pipe two balls to form bird heads. Set aside bag of orange.

**ACTUAL SIZE**

**6.** Attach tube 17 to a decorating bag; fill with blue. Pipe two shells to form the outer petals on the center tulip. Wash and dry tube 13; attach to bag of blue. Pipe two small shells to form the center of the red tulips. Pipe tube 13 blue drop flowers along green stems. Wash and dry tube 1; attach to bag of blue. Pipe bird tails and dots at base of heart.

**7.** Wash and dry tube 13; attach to a decorating bag and fill with yellow. Fill in bodies of birds with drop stars. Pipe tube 13 yellow drop flowers along green stems. Wash and dry tube 1; attach to bag of yellow. Pipe beak and eye on each bird head. Pipe yellow tube 1 dots in the center of orange and blue drop flowers. Pipe two dots along tulip stem and above the blue petals of the center tulip.

**8.** Wash and dry tube 1; attach to bag of orange. Pipe bird feet and a dot in the center of each yellow drop flower.

**9.** Frost sides of cake with yellow buttercream, using a small spatula to form curved ridges in the buttercream.

**10.** Wash and dry tube 6; attach to bag of yellow. Pipe ball border around top of cake. Transfer cake to serving platter of your choice. Pipe ball border around base of cake.

# Baby Booties Cake

Blue flowers for a boy, pink flowers for a girl. There is one of each on this cake, which is decorated for a baby shower. Change the message to "God Bless Baby" for a christening or "Happy Birthday" for baby's first. With gender no longer a question, pipe all flowers in the appropriate color, adding tiny green leaves to set them off.

## Preparing the cakes

*1 9- by 13-inch cake layer, cooled to room temperature and leveled*

*1 recipe Jam Glaze*

*8-inch square cardboard base, covered with parchment*

Note that a cake baked in a 9- by 13-inch pan measures about 8 by 12 inches when turned out.

**1.** Cut 8-inch square cake and bootie sections as illustrated.

**2.** Place cake sections on a rack and brush on warm jam glaze. Air-dry for about an hour, until set.

**3.** Transfer 8-inch square cake to prepared cardboard base using a bit of glaze or buttercream to secure in place. Assemble bootie sections; set aside.

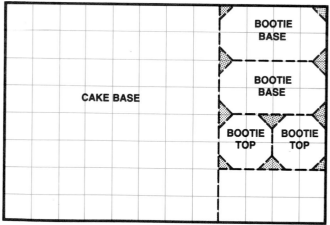

**EACH SQUARE EQUALS 1 INCH**
**CUT OFF AND DISCARD GRAY AREAS**

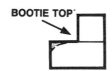

BOOTIE TOP

## Preparing the frosting

*1 recipe Classic Buttercream*

*Paste food colors: lemon yellow, pink, sky blue*

*Tubes: 2, 3, 4, 15, 17, 20, 225*

Mix and tint buttercream the day before or while waiting for glaze to set.

**1.** Tint one third of buttercream yellow. Place ½ cup yellow into a decorating bag fitted with tube 4. Cover remaining yellow with plastic wrap.

**2.** Tint ¼ cup buttercream blue; transfer to parchment cone fitted with tube 225.

**3.** Tint ¼ cup buttercream pink; cover with plastic.

**4.** Attach tube 15 to decorating bag; fill with white buttercream. Cover remaining white with plastic.

**5.** Set remaining tubes aside.

## Decorating the cake

*2 decorating bags, fitted with couplings*

*2 parchment cones*

**1.** Frost 8-inch square cake with yellow buttercream, spreading it as smoothly as possible. Transfer to serving platter.

**2.** Use a turntable to decorate one bootie at a time. Beginning at the top of bootie and working your way around it in rows, pipe white shells for a knitted affect with tube 15.

**3.** With tube 4, pipe yellow stitching around bootie; pipe bow. Attach tube 2 to bag of yellow; set aside.

**4.** Pipe tube 225 drop flowers in blue and pink. Pipe a tube 2 yellow dot in the center of each.

**5.** Transfer booties to cake top. Spread a layer of white buttercream, as smoothly as possible, over the top opening of each bootie. Attach tube 17 to bag of yellow; pipe shell border around top of booties.

**6.** Attach tube 3 to bag of white; pipe message.

**7.** Wash and dry tube 17; attach to bag of white. Pipe shell border around upper edge of square cake.

**8.** Attach tube 20 to bag of white; pipe shell border around base of cake.

# Mortarboard Graduation Cake

A rice-paper diploma tied with a marzipan bow and a tassel made with spaghettini strands tinted in school colors add a realistic touch to this clever two-tier graduation cake. Only a small amount of marzipan is needed to make the bow—if you don't have any on hand, make a full recipe and store what you don't use in the freezer. The decorations should be removed from the cake prior to serving.

Both cake tiers are frosted with chocolate buttercream, but the top tier has a final coating of chocolate fondant to give it a smooth shine.

## Preparing the decorations

*1 sheet rice paper*

*½ cup Marzipan (or Mock Marzipan)*

*1 egg white, lightly beaten*

*About 40 strands spaghettini (thin spaghetti)*

*Paste food colors: super red, royal blue, lemon yellow*

*4 tablespoons vegetable oil*

**1.** Carefully roll rice paper into a scroll. Place a rubber band about 2-inches in from each end to hold the roll in place. Set aside.

**2.** To make bow, tint ½ cup marzipan red. Roll marzipan into a circle ⅛-inch thick between two sheets of plastic wrap generously sprinkled with confectioners' sugar. Carefully peel off the top sheet of wrap; run a spatula under the marzipan to make sure that it hasn't stuck. Brush off excess sugar. Cut out an 8- by ⅜-inch strip of marzipan. Lift it off the plastic wrap; brush off excess sugar from underneath, then lay it in front of yourself. Lift both ends of the strip, bringing them over to meet at the center of the strip, then press the ends and the bottom strip firmly together, to form a bow. Use a bit of egg white as glue, if necessary, to hold the bow in place. Cut out a 2- by ⅜-inch strip of marzipan; wrap it over the top and sides of the seam in the bow, using a bit of egg white as glue. (Do not wrap the small strip completely around the bow; trim off the ends flush with the bottom of the bow so that it sits straight.) Gently spread the sides of the bow apart and place it on its side to dry.

**3.** Cut out a 7- by ⅜-inch marzipan strip; bursh off excess sugar. Place strip around center of scroll, sealing it at the bottom with a bit of egg white. Be careful not to get egg white onto the scroll itself, because this will cause it to wrinkle and soften. Do not remove rubber bands. Set scroll aside with the marzipan seam-side down.

**4.** To make tassel, fill two pans with 2 quarts of water each; bring to a boil. Place about 1 tablespoon of lemon yellow paste food color into one pan and about 2 teaspoons royal blue into the other. Cook half the spaghettini in the yellow water and half in the blue water, both for about 11 minutes.

**5.** Place 2 tablespoons vegetable oil into each of two small bowls. Remove tinted spaghettini from pans with a slotted spoon, placing the yellow strands in one bowl, the blue in the other. Stir to coat strands with oil.

**6.** Now construct an elevated rack on which to dry the strands. Place two tall cans of equal height at each end of a cookie sheet. Set a metal rack on top of the cans, so that it is elevated over the cookie sheet by at least 6 inches. Take a strand of spaghettini, holding it in the middle so that it bends in two, and hang it on the rack in a hair-pin position. Repeat procedure with all the strands, hanging the yellow on one side of the rack and the blue on the other, making sure that the strands do not touch each other or stick together. Air-dry for about 30 minutes. The excess oil with drip off the strands onto the cookie sheet.

**7.** Remove spaghettini strands from rack and place, still folded like hair pins, onto a paper towel; pat dry. Set aside about five strands of yellow and two strands of blue.

**8.** Hang the remaining strands in a group, alternating the colors over your left forefinger, to form the tassel. Lay the tassel in a neat pile on a table without disturbing the arrangement. Using two of the reserved strands, hook one yellow and one blue through

the center of the tassel arrangement to form a four-strand cord. Tighten the tassel around the cord by squeezing the bent strands at the tops of the tassel together.

**9.** Using another reserved yellow strand, wrap a coil around the tassel about 1 inch from the top. Moisten the coil with egg white to secure it in place.

**10.** Thread yet another yellow strand through the eye of the tassel. Holding one end of the strand at the point where the tassel and cord are hooked together, wrap a coil around the top of the tassel to cover the join. Moisten the coil with egg white to secure in place.

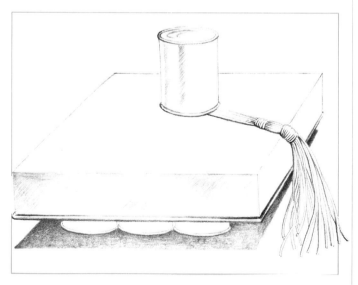

**11.** The completed tassel, with cord attached, must now be positioned on an inverted 9-inch square cake pan so that when completely dry, the tassel will hold its draped shape. Elevate the pan by standing a few tall cans of equal height underneath it. Lay the tassel on the pan in the same position that it will take when

placed upon the cake. Flatten the cord and trim the ends so that they reach only to the center of the pan when the tassel is in position. Use another can, in place of the coiled tassel button, to hold the ends of the cord in place. Moisten the cord with egg white to keep the strands aligned together. Using a pair of scissors, shorten and trim the ends of the tassel so that they will barely touch the serving platter when hanging from the cake.

**12.** To form the tassel button, wind a yellow spaghettini strand into a flat coil; moisten with egg white so that it will keep its shape. Set aside to dry.

## Preparing the cake

*1 8-inch square cake layer, cooled to room temperature and leveled*

*1 9-inch square cake layer, cooled to room temperature and leveled*

*1 recipe Jam Glaze*

*2 8-inch square cardboard bases*

*Parchment paper*

**1.** Using the diagram as a guide, shave off corners of an 8-inch square cake to form base of cap. Transfer to a rack, together with the 9-inch square layer and brush on warm jam glaze. Air-dry for about an hour, until set.

**2.** Prepare buttercream and fondant while waiting for glaze to set.

**3.** Cut one 8-inch square cardboard base to shape and size of bottom tier (base of cap); cover with parchment. Transfer cake to prepared cardboard base, securing it in place with a bit of buttercream. Transfer 9-inch cake layer to remaining cardboard base (uncovered), and secure with buttercream.

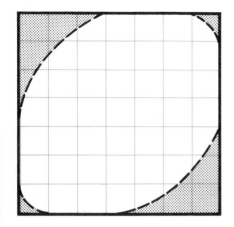

**EACH SQUARE EQUALS 1 INCH**

**CUT OFF AND DISCARD GRAY AREAS**

## Decorating the cake

*6 plastic drinking straws*

*1 recipe Classic Buttercream, chocolate*

*1 recipe Quick Fondant Icing, chocolate*

**1.** Frost top and sides of both tiers with chocolate buttercream, spreading it as smoothly as possible.

**2.** Transfer top tier (9-inch layer) to a rack placed over a cookie sheet. Pour warm fondant over cake, spreading fondant with a spatula to cover top and sides completely. Pierce air bubbles with a straight pin as soon as they form.

**3.** To assemble the cake, plastic drinking straws must be cut to the exact height of the bottom tier to support the weight of the top tier once they are stacked upon each other. The bottom tier has six straw supports. Following the shape of the cake, insert the straws equidistant from each other and about 1½ inches from the outer edge of the cake. Make a pencil mark on the straws where they meet the top of the frosting. Remove straws; determine which has the lowest pencil mark, and cut just slightly below the mark. Line up the remaining five straws; cut them the same length as the first. Replace cut straws in cake.

**4.** Transfer bottom tier to serving platter of your choice, using a small amount of buttercream to secure it in place. Position the square tier on top of the base, lining one of its corners up with a pointed side of the bottom tier.

**5.** Use a bit of egg white to attach marzipan bow to ribbon wrapped around scroll. The bow will make the decoration top-heavy and it will want to roll over. Prop a small ball of marzipan behind the scroll to keep it upright.

**6.** The fondant should still be tacky enough to hold the decorations in place. Transfer the tassel to the top of the cake, slightly pressing it in place. Place the tassel button over the end of the cord at the center of the cake. Place scroll tied with bow on top of cake. If necessary, place a small ball of marzipan behind it to keep it from rolling over.

# Strawberry Basket

What better way to celebrate the arrival of spring—or even Valentine's Day—than with marzipan strawberries and heart-shaped leaves adorning a cake of woven buttercream. Patience rather than skill are the key words here, but rave results will make the time spent all worth while. This basket of sweetness can, of course, be embellished with other kinds of fruits for other occasions.

## Preparing the marzipan or mock marzipan

*1 recipe Marzipan or Mock Marzipan*

*Special tools: food grater, rolling pin, ½-inch star-shaped aspic cutter, ½-inch and 1-inch heart-shaped aspic cutters, 2-inch heart-shaped cookie cutter, artist's brush*

*1 egg white, lightly beaten*

*Paste food colors: red, green*

**1.** Using red food color, tint about ½ cup marzipan pink. To make strawberries, pinch off a small amount of marzipan and roll it into a ball between the palms of your hands. (Each ball should be slightly different in size, ranging from ¾- to 1¼-inch in diameter.) Roll the ball into a strawberry shape over a food grater to give it texture. Place on a tray lined with waxed paper; air-dry several hours.

**2.** Using green food coloring, tint about ½ cup marzipan pale green. To make leaves and strawberry caps, roll marzipan into a circle ⅛-inch thick between two sheets of plastic wrap generously sprinkled with confectioners' sugar. Carefully peel off the top sheet of wrap; run a long spatula underneath the marzipan circle to make sure that it hasn't stuck. Brush off excess sugar.

**3.** Cut several heart-shaped leaves with the cookie and aspic cutters; transfer them with a spatula to a tray lined with waxed paper. Use star-shaped aspic cutter to cut strawberry caps. Remove them from the wrap one at a time, dab one side with a drop of egg white and press the cap onto a strawberry. The egg white acts as a glue.

## Preparing the cake

*2 8- or 9-inch round cake layers, cooled to room temperature and leveled*

*1 recipe Jam Glaze*

*1 7- or 8-inch round cardboard base, covered with parchment*

**1.** Place cake layers on a rack; brush on warm jam glaze, then air-dry for about an hour.

**2.** Transfer one cake layer to the prepared cardboard base using a bit of glaze or buttercream to secure in place. Spread a thin layer of white buttercream over the top, then position top layer.

## Preparing the frosting

*1 recipe Classic Buttercream*

*Paste food colors: green, malt brown, lemon yellow*

Mix and tint buttercream the day before or while waiting for glaze to set.

**1.** Place ¼ cup buttercream into each of two small bowls; tint one bowl green and the other yellow. Cover each with plastic wrap.

**2.** Using brown food color and a speck of yellow, tint two-thirds of the remaining buttercream beige. Cover with plastic wrap. Cover remaining white buttercream with plastic wrap.

## Decorating the cake

*Tubes: 2, 4, 48, 225*

*2 decorating bags, fitted with couplings*

*2 parchment cones*

*Light corn syrup*

*Paste food color: red*

**1.** Fit a decorating bag with tube 4 and fill with white buttercream. Beginning at any point around the cake, pipe a straight line from the top edge to the base.

**2.** Fit a decorating bag with tube 48 and fill with beige buttercream. Pipe horizontal slats over the white line from top to bottom, a tube width apart. (See basket-weave technique on page 39). Repeat procedure with white and beige to cover the side of the cake. To make basket-weave on top of cake, pipe white line from center of cake towards the edge. Pipe beige slats over the white line, a tube width apart. Those near the center of the cake are very short, increasing in length towards the edge of the cake. Cover entire cake top in basket-weave pattern.

**3.** Insert tube 2 in a parchment cone and fill with green buttercream. Pipe spray of stems on top of cake.

**4.** Arrange strawberries and leaves off the spray of stems. Pipe a green tube 2 dot on top of each strawberry cap. Wash and dry tube 2.

**5.** Attach tube 225 to bag of white buttercream. Pipe drop flowers.

**6.** Insert tube 2 in a parchment cone and fill with yellow buttercream. Pipe a dot at the center of each drop flower.

**7.** Thin about 3 tablespoons of corn syrup with a few drops of very hot water. Tint with red food color. Use an artist's brush to paint red glaze over strawberries.

# Happy Hatchback Car

Give a lift to a birthday child who loves cars or perhaps to a special someone who has just acquired their first driving license or a new job working as an auto mechanic. To make the cake even more amusing and memorable, cut out a snapshot of the person that you are honoring (head and shoulders only, about 1½ inches in height) and attach it to the windshield (driver's side) with a dab of buttercream. Similar size photos of party guests or a favorite pet may also be attached to the window areas where passengers would be seated. If decorating with photographs, don't bother to pipe the windshield wipers and remember to remove the photos prior to serving the cake.

Two 11- by- 17 by 1-inch sheet cakes have to be baked in order to construct this sporty little hatchback, and because only part of the second cake is needed, you will have some leftover. Once assembled, the car is fairly easy to decorate since most of the work is done with a star tube. The windows are pre-frosted with buttercream and then spread with a shiny second coat of buttercream mixed with an equal amount of piping gel. Look at the reflection in the rear-view mirror to decorate the back of the car.

## Preparing the cake

*2 11- by 17- by 1-inch cake layers, cooled to room temperature and leveled*

*1 recipe Jam Glaze*

*5½- by 10-inch cardboard base, covered with parchment*

Note that a cake baked in an 11- by- 17-inch pan measures about 10 by 16 inches when turned out. Because this cake consists of five layers, each layer must be perfectly level for the cake to stand straight.

**1.** Cut one cake layer into three equal sections, measuring 5½ by 10 by 1 inch each. Cut second cake layer into equal sections, measuring 5½ by 6½ by 1 inch. The rest of the cake will not be needed; store accordingly.

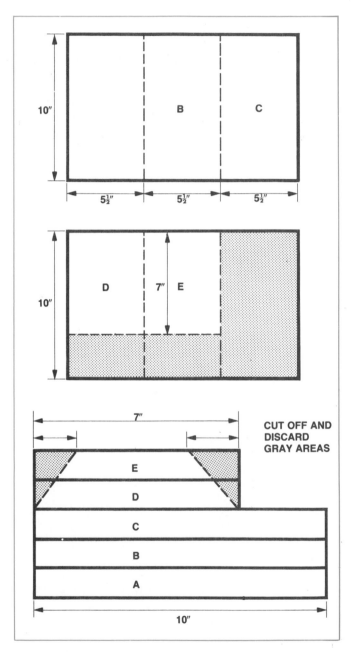

**2.** Assemble cake sections as shown in diagram. Cut off and discard the corner pieces of sections D and E to shape a slanted windshield and hatchback for the car. Disassemble cake sections and transfer them to a rack. Brush on warm jam glaze, then air-dry for about an hour, until set.

**3.** Transfer section A to cardboard base, using a thin layer of white buttercream to secure it in place. Stack remaining layers on top of first, spreading a thin, even layer of white buttercream filling between each.

## Preparing the frosting

*1½ recipes Classic Buttercream*

*Clear piping gel*

*Paste food colors: sky blue, orange, super red, black, lemon yellow*

Mix and tint buttercream the day before or while waiting for glaze to set.

**1.** Mix a ½ recipe of buttercream and tint it lemon yellow. Attach tube 4 to a decorating bag; fill with yellow; set aside. Cover remaining yellow with plastic wrap.

**2.** Mix a full recipe of buttercream. Tint 1½ cups pale sky blue; cover with plastic wrap.

**3.** Place ¼ cup buttercream into each of three small bowls. Tint one bowl orange, one bowl red, and one bowl light gray; cover with plastic wrap.

**4.** Tint ½ cup buttercream dark gray. (It will turn black when it dries.) Cover with plastic wrap.

**5.** Cover remaining white buttercream with plastic wrap.

## Decorating the cake

*Tubes: 2, 4, 6, 15, 18*

*4 decorating bags, fitted with couplings*

*2 parchment cones*

**1.** Frost all around the sides of sections D and E with a thin layer of pale blue buttercream, spreading it as smoothly as possible. Beat an equal amount of piping gel into the remaining blue buttercream. Spread mixture as evenly as you can over the first layer of blue buttercream.

**2.** Frost all around the sides of section A, B and C with a smooth layer of white buttercream.

**3.** Use the edge of a long spatula to mark off straight lines outlining the windows, hood, doors and base of car. Using tube 4, pipe yellow lines along markings, allowing a semicircular space for each tire. Wash and dry tube 4.

**4.** Using a toothpick, mark the outline of two headlights within the grill area. Fill a decorating bag with light gray buttercream; attach tube 4. Pipe grill lines and outline of license plate. Attach tube 6 to bag of light gray; pipe front and rear bumpers.

**5.** Fill a decorating bag with red buttercream; attach tube 2. Pipe name on license plate. Attach tube 15 to bag of red. Pipe red stars to resemble rear break lights.

**6.** Wash and dry tube 15; insert into a parchment cone and fill with orange. Pipe orange stars to resemble side and rear signal lights.

**7.** Attach tube 18 to bag of yellow. Pipe yellow stars to fill in body of car.

**8.** Wash and dry tube 2; attach to bag of light gray. Pipe spokes, door handles, rearview mirror, windshield wipers (if not using photographs) and outline of headlights.

**9.** Wash and dry tube 15; insert into a parchment cone and fill with white buttercream. Pipe stars for headlights.

**10.** Wash and dry tube 18. Attach to a decorating bag and fill with dark gray (black). Pipe tires. Wash and dry tube 6; attach to bag of dark gray. Transfer cake to serving platter of your choice. Pipe a dark gray caulking line around base of car.

**11.** Cut out and mount photographs, if using.

# Fun-in-the-Sunglasses Cake

Create a spectacle by serving a pair of rose-tinted sunglasses at a summer party by the pool or beach. Or, decorate it as a sendoff when your daughter goes to camp or when someone special leaves for a sunny vacation. Silver dragées add a realistic touch. Although they're edible, I suggest removing them from the cake before serving since they're hard and most unpleasant to bite into.

## Preparing the cake

2 9-inch square cake layers, cooled to room temperature and leveled

1 recipe Jam Glaze

2 8-inch square cardboard bases

Parchment paper

Note that a cake baked in a 9-inch square pan measures about 8 inches square when turned out.

1. Draw a pattern for one sunglass frame onto a sheet of parchment or waxed paper. Cut out pattern. Place pattern onto one cake layer; cut out cake. *Reverse pattern* and place on other cake layer; cut out opposite frame. Cut a slightly curved nose piece, about 1 by 1½ inches, from the scrap cake.

2. Place cake sections on a rack. Brush on warm jam glaze, then allow to set for about an hour.

3. Trace cake pattern for each section onto cardboard; cut cardboard to size. Cover with parchment. Transfer cake sections to appropriate-sized cardboard sections, using a bit of glaze or buttercream to secure in place.

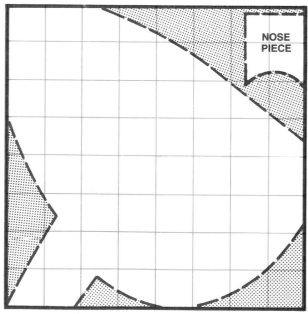

NOSE PIECE

**EACH SQUARE EQUALS 1 INCH**
**CUT OFF AND DISCARD GRAY AREAS**

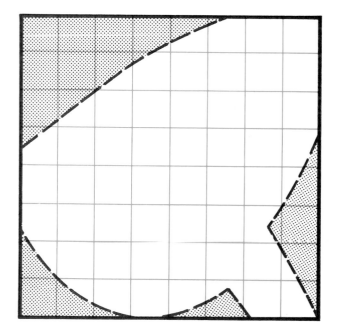

## Preparing the frosting

*1 recipe Classic Buttercream*
*½ cup clear piping gel*
*Paste food colors: pink, sky blue, green*
*Tubes 2, 4, 8, 10*

Mix and tint buttercream the day before or while waiting for glaze to set.

**1.** Tint 2 cups buttercream pink. Transfer 1½ cups to decorating bag fitted with tube 10. Add piping gel to remaining ½ cup of pink buttercream to give a gloss; cover with plastic wrap.

**2.** Tint ¼ cup buttercream blue. Transfer to parchment cone fitted with tube 8.

**3.** Tint ¼ cup buttercream green. Cover with plastic wrap. Cover remaining buttercream with plastic wrap.

**4.** Set remaining tubes aside.

## Decorating the cake

*8 medium-sized silver dragées*
*1 decorating bag, fitted with a coupling*
*3 parchment cones*
*10- by 20-inch serving tray*

Frost the cake sections separately; transfer them to the serving tray; seal seams with frosting.

**1.** Frost top and sides of one frame with white buttercream spreading it as smoothly as possible.

**2.** With tube 10, pipe pink lens using an outline and fill-in technique. Smooth with a hot spatula. Spread a smooth layer of glossy pink (buttercream and gel mixture) over the pink lens to give it a shine. Attach tube 4 to bag of pink; pipe a caulking line around the lens. Transfer frame to serving tray. Repeat procedure 1 and 2 with the other frame.

**3.** Frost top and sides of nose piece with white. Transfer to serving tray. Smooth seams with a hot spatula.

**4.** Place ¼ cup white buttercream into a parchment cone fitted with tube 2. Pipe a line to separate the frames of the glasses from the ear pieces. Pipe name on lens.

**5.** With tube 8, pipe random dots of blue over frames and ear pieces. Wash and dry tube 8.

**6.** Insert tube 8 into a parchment cone; fill with green. Pipe random tube 8 dots of green.

**7.** Position silver dragées on cake with a tweezer. Press them down slightly so that they won't roll off.

# Holiday Cakes

VALENTINE'S DAY

SAINT PATRICK'S DAY

EASTER

MOTHER'S DAY

FATHER'S DAY

INDEPENDENCE DAY

HALLOWEEN

THANKSGIVING

CHRISTMAS/WASHINGTON'S
BIRTHDAY

NEW YEAR'S EVE

# Valentine's Chocolate Romance Cake

If it's true that the way to a man's heart is through his stomach, this voluptuous Chocolate Romance Cake should have him eating right out of your hands. As sensational as it looks, you'll be suprised at how easy it is to decorate. The rich chocolate glaze is simply poured over the cake and then stroked into sensuous curves. The scarlet roses are made in advance. (Because their intense coloring imparts a bitter flavor, they should be removed from the cake prior to serving.) The Shaved Chocolate Bark is also easily made in advance, and the leaves take only minutes. If you're going to present the cake in a warm room, keep it refrigerated until serving. The cake in the photograph was baked in a 12-inch heart-shaped pan, but an equally lovely heart-shaped cake can be created by baking one 8-inch round layer and one 8-inch square layer and assembling them as illustrated for the Loving Heart Cake on page 164.

## Preparing the decorations

*1 recipe Royal Icing or Bette's Decoration Buttercream, stiffened*

*Flower Nail*

*Paste food colors: super Christmas red, violet*

*Tube: 124*

*1 decorating bag (see note)*

*1 recipe Shaved Chocolate Bark*

*12 fresh, medium-sized rose leaves*

*Note: Tube 124 is very large and can't be used with a coupling. Simply insert it into the decorating bag.*

1. Using super red and just a speck of violet, tint stiffened royal icing or buttercream scarlet. Pipe several scarlet roses with tube 124. Air-dry and store until needed. (You will need four of the best.)
2. Prepare Shaved Chocolate Bark according to recipe and refrigerate until needed.
3. Prepare about 12 chocolate leaves according to the recipe. Refrigerate until needed.

## Preparing the cake

*1 12- by 2-inch heart-shaped cake layer, cooled to room temperature and leveled.*

*1 recipe Jam Glaze*

*12-inch cardboard base, cut to size of heart cake and covered with parchment*

1. Place cake on rack. Brush on warm jam glaze, then air-dry for about an hour, until set.
2. Transfer cake to prepared cardboard base, using a bit of jam glaze to secure it in place. Return cake to rack placed over a clean baking sheet.

## Decorating the cake

*1 recipe Rich Chocolate Glaze*

1. Prepare recipe for Rich Chocolate Glaze. While warm, pour it over the cake. Use a spatula to smooth it around the sides of the cake and then stroke the top of the cake with the tip of the spatula to form ridges similar to those shown in the photograph. Glaze that drips onto the baking sheet can be scraped up and used again.
2. Remove Shaved Chocolate Bark from the refrigerator and crush it slightly in your hand. Press the bark onto the sides of the cake. The chocolate glaze should be tacky enough to hold it in place. Transfer cake to serving platter of your choice.
3. Arrange three roses on top of cake and place one at its base.
4. Using a teaspoon, scrape up a small amount of chocolate glaze from the baking pan. It should be cool enough to hold its shape when rolled into a small ball. If not, refrigerate until it can be handled. Prepare about 6 small chocolate balls to be used as props underneath the chocolate leaves, to hold them up at an angle.
5. Remove chocolate leaves from refrigerator. Starting at the stem end, carefully separate leaves from chocolate. Try to handle the leaves as little as possible, and quickly arrange the best ones next to the roses, using the small chocolate balls to prop them up and secure them in place.
6. Refrigerate cake until presentation time. Remove roses and arrange them on the serving platter prior to serving the cake.

# Shamrock Cake

Tiny royal-icing shamrocks adorn this cheerful Saint Patrick's Day cake and provide just the right touch of traditional Kelly green. The printing and shell borders are piped with buttercream in a softer shade of Kelly green which adds a nice color balance and better flavor appeal. (If buttercream is tinted too deeply, it tends to taste bitter and often stains one's mouth and teeth.)

Irish coffee is the perfect cake accompaniment on this fun-filled holiday. To decorate, dip the rims of the coffee mugs or glasses, one at a time, into a saucer containing a shallow depth of green cream de menthe, then into a saucer containing granulated sugar. The sugared rims can be prepared several hours in advance. When ready to serve, carefully pour in the whiskey and coffee and top with whipped cream piped from a decorating bag with a large star tube attached.

## Preparing the decorations

*1 recipe Royal Icing*
*Paste food color: Kelly green*
*Tube: 2*

1. Prepare royal icing and tint Kelly green. Attach tube 2 to a decorating bag and fill with tinted icing.
2. To make shamrocks, pipe a series of small hearts, formed by joining two small tube 2 shells together. The work may be done on a sheet of waxed paper placed over a cookie sheet for support. You will need at least 100 small hearts to form the leaves on each side of the shamrocks. The central leaf is formed by piping a tail, about ¼-inch long at the base of a tube 2 heart. You will need at least 50 central leaves with tails attached. Air-dry until hard, at least three hours, or overnight.

## Preparing the cake

*1 9- by 13-inch cake layer, cooled to room temperature and leveled*

*1 recipe Jam Glaze*
*9- by 13-inch cardboard cake base, covered with parchment*

1. Place cake layer on a rack. Brush on warm jam glaze, then air-dry for about an hour, until set.
2. Transfer cake to prepared cardboard base, using a bit of jam glaze or buttercream to secure it in place.

## Decorating the cake

*1 recipe Classic Buttercream*
*Paste food colors: Kelly green, lemon yellow*
*Tubes: 2, 4, 15, 20*
*1 decorating bag, fitted with a coupling*
*1 parchment cone*

Mix and tint buttercream the day before or while waiting for glaze to set.

1. Tint ½ cup buttercream yellow. Transfer to a parchment cone fitted with tube 4.
2. Tint 1½ cups buttercream a medium shade of Kelly green. Attach tube 2 to a decorating bag; fill with green. Cover remaining green with plastic wrap.
3. Cover white buttercream with plastic wrap.
4. Frost the sides and top of the cake with white buttercream, spreading it as smoothly as possible.
5. Measure and divide the length of the cake into five equal sections. Use a long spatula to mark the dividing lines in the frosting. Place center leaves of shamrocks on cake; place a small green heart on each side of the stems to form shamrocks.
6. Pipe message, using tube 2 green buttercream.
7. Attach tube 15 to bag of green; pipe connecting shells along the dividing lines. Pipe tube 4 yellow lines along both sides of the green shells.
8. Pipe a tube 15 green shell border around top edge of cake. Transfer cake to serving platter of your choice. Attach tube 20 to bag of green; pipe a shell border around base of cake.

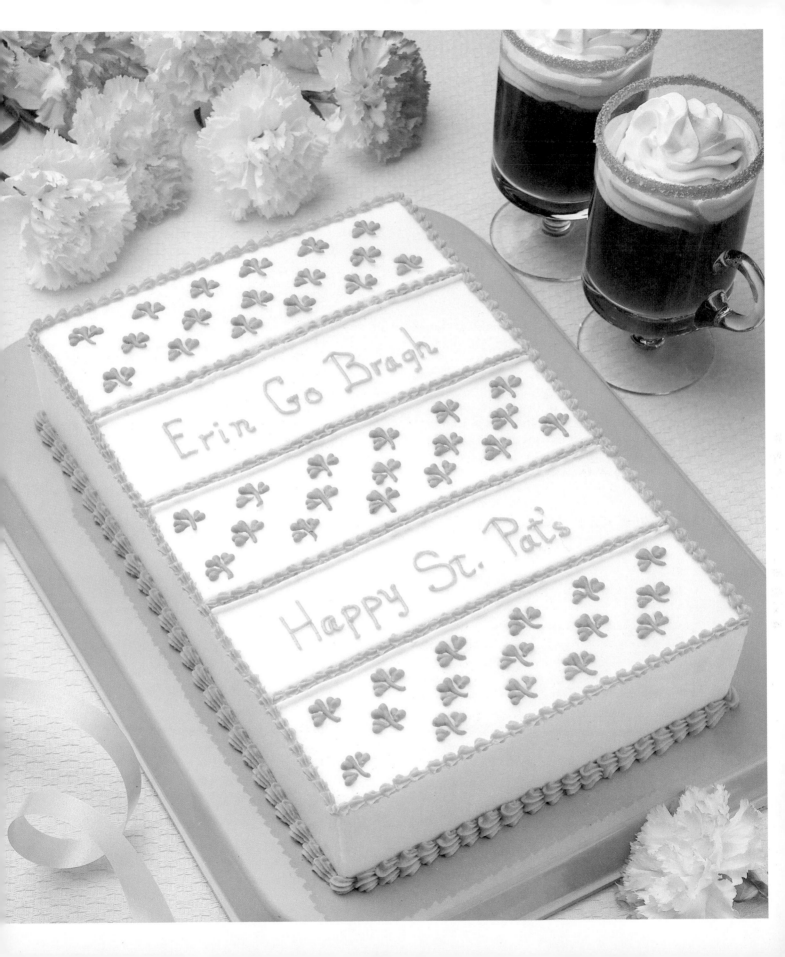

# Happy Easter Cake

If you have ever tried to decorate a large egg-shaped cake, you know that it is extremely tedious to ice it from the top to bottom with a silky smooth layer of buttercream. Covering it with poured fondant would seem an easier solution, but gravity and air currents work against the odd-shaped cake, so that the fondant usually ends up with a lumpy surface, making the cake look more like a bruised brain than a delicate egg.

The Easter cake presented here looks as though its top were covered with fondant, but actually, it has been frosted with a tasty mixture of buttercream and piping gel, which spreads quite easily. By decorating the bottom half of the cake with a star tube applied in the basket-weave technique, the graceful egg shape is accentuated and made to look even more interesting. The narcissis and forsythia blossoms are piped in advance from Royal Icing. (See pages 54 and 55.)

## Preparing the cake

*2 cake layers baked in an egg-shaped pan, cooled to room temperature*

*1 recipe Jam Glaze*

**1.** Level cake layers so that they will fit together. Cut a slice from underneath the bottom layer so that the cake will stand straight when assembled.

**2.** Place cake layers on a rack. Brush warm jam glaze over the outside of the layers, then air-dry for about an hour, until set.

**3.** Assemble cake by spreading a thin layer of white buttercream between the layers.

## Preparing the frosting

*1 recipe Classic Buttercream*

*½ cup clear piping gel*

*Paste food colors: lemon yellow, green*

*Tubes: 2, 6, 16, 20, 65s*

*2 decorating bags, fitted with couplings*

*1 parchment cone*

Mix and tint buttercream the day before or while waiting for glaze to set.

**1.** Tint ¼ cup buttercream green; transfer to a decorating bag fitted with tube 65s.

**2.** Insert tube 6 into the parchment cone; fill with 1 cup white buttercream.

**3.** Tint 1½ cups buttercream pale lemon yellow. Place ½ cup of pale yellow into a bowl; add ½ cup of clear piping gel and stir to mix. Cover bowls with plastic wrap.

**4.** Tint remaining buttercream a medium shade of lemon yellow. Transfer to a decorating bag fitted with tube 20; cover remaining medium yellow with plastic wrap.

## Decorating the cake

*2 Royal Icing narcissus*

*12 Royal Icing forsythia blossoms*

**1.** Spread a thin layer of pale lemon yellow buttercream over the entire surface of the cake, frosting the top smoothly and slightly thicker than the bottom.

**2.** Frost the top half of the egg with the pale yellow buttercream-gel mixture, spreading it as smoothly as possible. Using a knife, draw a line midway around the egg and remove any excess buttercream-gel mixture below the line.

**3.** Using tube 6 white lines and tube 20 medium yellow shells, pipe basket-weave pattern around base of cake.

**4.** Attach tube 16 to bag of medium yellow; pipe shell border around upper edge of basket weave.

**5.** Pipe message with tube 65s green. Place narcissus on cake, attach tube 2 to bag of green; pipe stems on message and both sides of narcissus. Arrange forsythia blossoms along stems. Attach tube 65s to bag of green; pipe ferns and tiny leaves at base of each forsythia blossom.

# Basket of Daisies Cake for Mother's Day

Surprise! Here's a cake that doesn't require leveling. In fact, the higher it mounds, the more attractive it will look when decorated. Hence the use of an 8-inch square cake pan which generally mounds higher than any other. A small ledge is removed from the edge of the cake to make room for the rope border at the top of the basket decoration. The daisies and drop flowers are piped in buttercream directly onto the bed of buttercream leaves, but if preferred, they can just as easily be piped in advance with royal icing. (Decoration Buttercream is not recommended for piping daisies in advance, because their fragile petals might break during transfer.) The leaves are piped in two shades of green. Thus, two parchment cones cut into the shape of large leaf tubes are required, unless you own and prefer to use two metal tube 70s simultaneously. Directions for cutting a parchment cone into a leaf shape are given on page 33. Although this makes an ideal cake for Mother's Day, it is so charming that you will no doubt think of many other occasions to decorate it.

## Preparing the cake

*1 8-inch square cake layer, cooled to room temperature*

*1 recipe Jam Glaze*

*8-inch square cardboard base, covered with parchment*

**1.** Refer to diagram, then cut a wedge, about ⅜ inch deep, all around the edge of the cake.

**2.** Transfer cake to a rack; brush on warm jam glaze, then air-dry for about an hour, until set.

**3.** Transfer glazed cake to prepared cardboard base, using a bit of glaze or buttercream to secure it in place.

## Preparing the Frosting

*1½ recipes Classic Buttercream*

*⅓ cup unsweetened cocoa*

*2 tablespoons butter, softened*

*2 teaspoons (approximately) milk*

*Paste food colors: egg yellow, malt brown, lemon yellow, orange, green*

*Tubes: 1, 6, 13, 20, 98, 150, 225, (two 70s optional)*

*4 decorating bags, fitted with couplings*

*3 parchment cones*

Mix and tint buttercream the day before or while waiting for glaze to set.

**1.** Tint about ¼ cup buttercream orange. Transfer to decorating bag fitted with tube 225.

**2.** Tint about ½ cup buttercream lemon yellow. Cover with plastic wrap.

**3.** Cut two parchment cones into the shape of a large leaf tube, or insert tube 70 into each of two parchment cones. Tint ¾ cup buttercream medium green; transfer to one parchment cone. Tint about ½ cup buttercream paler green; transfer to other parchment cone.

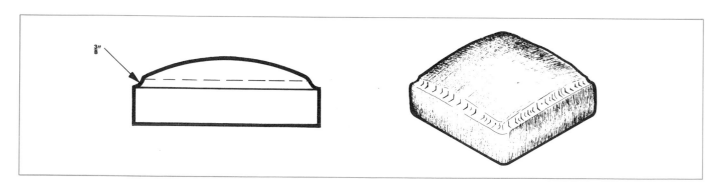

**4.** Using egg yellow with a bit of malt brown and just a speck of orange, tint about 3 cups buttercream gold. Attach tube 98 to a decorating bag and fill with gold buttercream. Cover remaining gold with plastic wrap.

**5.** Measure about 1½ cups buttercream into a mixing bowl. Add cocoa, butter and milk and beat until fluffy. Transfer to a decorating bag fitted with tube 6. Cover remaining chocolate with plastic wrap.

**6.** Insert tube 150 into a parchment cone; fill with white buttercream. Cover remaining white with plastic wrap.

## Decorating the cake

**1.** Using tube 98 with gold and tube 6 with chocolate, pipe a basket-weave decoration around the sides of the cake.

**2.** Attach tube 20 to bag of gold. To make handle, pipe one tube 20 line from the center of one side of the cake to the opposite side. (The single line is merely to give the handle more height.) Using tube 20 and firm pressure, pipe connecting reverse shells to form a rope over the single gold line. Using tube 20 and gentler pressure, pipe connecting reverse shells to form a rope around the cut out ledge at the edge of the cake.

**3.** Using leaf-shaped parchment cones, pipe leaves in two shades of green over the remaining surface of the cake, covering it entirely.

**4.** Wash and dry tube 6; attach to a decorating bag and fill with lemon yellow. To make daisies, pipe yellow centers at random positions over the bed of leaves. Pipe tube 150 white petals around each yellow center, working from the center outward.

**5.** Pipe a few tube 225 orange drop flowers in between the daisies. Attach tube 13 to bag of lemon yellow. Pipe a tiny yellow star on top of each orange drop flower, then pipe a few yellow stars on the bed of leaves.

**6.** Attach tube 1 to bag of orange. Pipe a dot in the center of each yellow star flower.

**7.** If necessary, pipe a few additional green leaves to balance the flower arrangement.

# Cake for the Sharpest Dad

Dad will be pleased to know that you think he's so keen when you present him with this delicious creation on Father's Day or his birthday. In fact, so would any other fellow—husband, son, brother, boyfriend, etc. Simply change the word 'Dad' to whomever you wish to honor.

## Preparing the cake

*1 9- by 13- by 2-inch cake layer, cooled to room temperature and leveled*

*1 recipe Jam Glaze*

*1 8- by 14-inch cardboard base*

*Parchment paper*

Note that a cake baked in a 9- by 13-inch pan measures about 8 by 12 inches when turned out.

**1.** Cut two inches off the width of the cake so that it measures 6 by 12 inches. (You will not need the 2- by 12-inch slice for this cake.) Following the diagram, cut the outer edges of the cake into the shape of a saw. (Do not cut out center of handle.)

**2.** Place cake on rack; brush on warm jam glaze, then air-dry for about an hour, until glaze is set.

**3.** Cut cardboard base to size of saw; cover with parchment. Transfer cake to prepared cardboard base, using a bit of glaze or buttercream to secure it in place.

## Preparing the frosting

*½ recipe Classic Buttercream*

*Paste food colors: navy or royal blue, egg yellow, malt brown, black*

*Tubes: 1, 3, 4, 6*

*1 decorating bag, fitted with a coupling*

*2 parchment cones*

Mix and tint buttercream the day before or while waiting for the glaze to set.

**1.** Tint about one third of the buttercream pale blue; cover with plastic wrap.

**2.** Using egg yellow and a bit of brown, tint half the remaining buttercream tan; cover with plastic wrap.

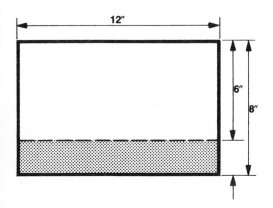

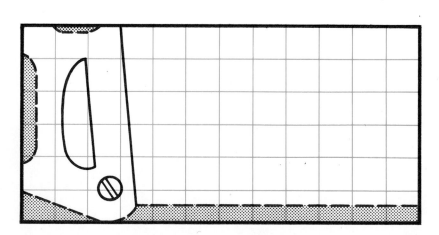

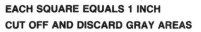

**EACH SQUARE EQUALS 1 INCH**
**CUT OFF AND DISCARD GRAY AREAS**

**3.** Tint ½ cup buttercream brownish-black; transfer to a decorating bag fitted with tube 4.

**4.** Transfer remaining white buttercream to a paper cone; snip the point off the cone, making a hole about the size of tube 6 for an opening.

## Decorating the cake

**1.** Frost the sides and top of the blade-end of the cake with pale blue. Use a hot spatula to smooth the surface as evenly as possible. Transfer remaining blue buttercream to a paper cone fitted with tube 6, and pipe a blue line around the base of the blade-end of the cake. Now, snip off the pointed end of the cone containing tube 6; wash and dry the tube.

**2.** Frost the sides and top of the handle-end of the cake with tan, spreading it as smoothly as possible.

**3.** Using cone of white, pipe an outline for the center of the handle, the teeth and the white portion of the eyes. Fill in the outlines, then smooth and flatten the white areas with a hot spatula.

**4.** Tint about a tablespoon of the remaining white buttercream yellow. Place it directly into tube 6 (without a bag or cone) and using your finger, force the buttercream through the tube to form a yellow bead (the screw) at the bottom left corner of the handle. Tap the head flat with a dampened finger. Wash and dry tube 6.

**5.** Using brownish-black and tube 4, outline the handle of the saw and pipe a zig-zag line down one side of the blade. Switch to tube 3 and pipe the facial details and outline the screw. Attach tube 6 and pipe a line around the base of the handle. Finally, change to tube 1 and print the message.

# Stars and Stripes Cake

Your family and friends will be filled with the spirit of Old Glory when you serve this patriotic cake on the Fourth of July. The star-shaped cake adds a symbolic touch, but if you don't own a star-shaped cake pan, the flag design can just as easily be piped onto the top of a round, square or rectangular-shaped cake. Simply frost about a third of the cake blue, then pipe the red and white stripes with tube 48 over the remaining surface.

## Preparing the cake

*1 star-shaped cake layer, cooled to room temperature and leveled*

*1 recipe Jam Glaze*

*Star-shaped cardboard base, cut to size of cake and covered with parchment*

1. Place cake on a rack. Brush on warm jam glaze, then air-dry for about an hour, until set.
2. Transfer cake to prepared cardboard base.

## Preparing the frosting

*1 recipe Classic Buttercream*

*Paste food colors: royal blue, super navy blue, super Christmas red*

*Tubes: 2, 4, 48, 98*

*2 decorating bags, fitted with couplings*

Mix and tint buttercream the day before or while waiting for glaze to set.

1. Tint about 1½ cups buttercream flag blue by mixing royal and navy blue and adding a very small amount of red. Be careful not to add too much red, or the color will take on a purple tone. Cover with plastic wrap.

2. Tint 1 cup buttercream red. Transfer to a decorating bag and place a small piece of waxed paper over the open coupling to keep the buttercream from crusting. (Remove paper before attaching tube to coupling.)

## Decorating the cake

1. Spread blue buttercream as smoothly as possible over top of cake, covering the area as shown in the photograph. Use a knife to remove excess blue from edge and center portion of cake, so that the frosting finishes in a smooth line.

ACTUAL SIZE

2. Measure the edge of the blue frosting and use a toothpick to mark the width of the red and white stripes. Pipe lengthways rows of tube 48, serrated side up, white stripes in the appropriate area. Use a knife to trim excess frosting from edge of cake.
3. Wash and dry tube 48; attach to bag of red and pipe red stripes. Trim excess frosting from edge of cake.
4. Frost sides of cake with white buttercream, spreading it as smoothly as possible.
5. Attach tube 2 to bag of white. Using the illustrated star pattern as a guide to size, pipe stars over blue area.
6. Attach tube 4 to bag of white; pipe a line to separate the blue area from the red and white striped area. Transfer cake to serving platter of your choice. Pipe a tube 4 caulking line around base of cake.
7. Attach tube 98 to bag of white; pipe border around upper edge of cake.

# Chocolate Halloween Bat

**On Halloween, treat guests to a cake masquerading as a bewitching chocolate bat. No tricks here—the cake is frightfully easy to cut and assemble; the decorations are piped lines and drop stars.**

## Preparing the cake

*1 9- by 13-inch cake layer, cooled to room temperature and leveled*

*1 recipe Jam Glaze*

Note that a cake baked in a 9- by 13-inch pan measures about 8 by 12 inches when turned out.

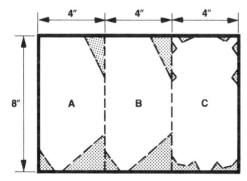

**EACH SQUARE EQUALS 1 INCH**
**CUT OFF AND DISCARD GRAY AREAS**

**1.** Cut cake into three 4- by 8-inch pieces. Using the illustration as a guide, draw a paper pattern for the wings and body sections. Cut out patterns; place on cake pieces; cut cake.

**2.** Transfer cake parts to a rack. Brush on warm jam glaze, then air-dry for about an hour, until set.

## Preparing the frosting

*1 recipe Classic Buttercream*

*¾ cup unsweetened cocoa*

*3 tablespoons butter, softened*

*1 tablespoon vegetable shortening*

*⅛ teaspoon salt*

*Several teaspoons milk*

*Paste food colors: lime green, lavender, orange*

*Tubes: 2, 4, 6, 13, 17*

*3 decorating bags, fitted with couplings*

*3 parchment cones*

Mix and tint buttercream the day before or while waiting for glaze to set.

**1.** Tint ¼ cup buttercream lime green. Transfer to a parchment cone fitted with tube 6.

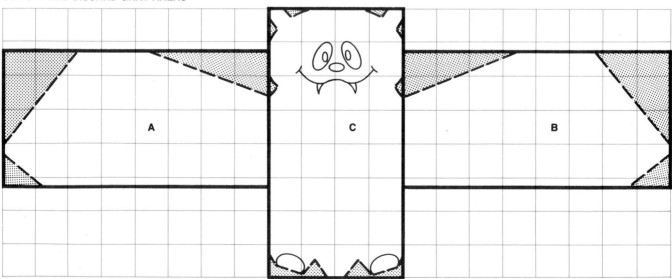

**2.** Tint ¼ cup buttercream lavender. Transfer to a parchment cone fitted with tube 4.

**3.** Tint 1 cup buttercream orange. Cover with plastic wrap.

**4.** Set aside ½ cup white buttercream. Cover with plastic wrap.

**5.** Add cocoa, butter, shortening, salt and 1 tablespoon milk to remaining buttercream. Beat until light and fluffy, adding additional milk to thin, if necessary. Attach tube 2 to a decorating bag and fill with chocolate.

**6.** Using ¼ cup of the white buttercream that was set aside, add a small amount of chocolate buttercream, mixing to a light beige color. Cover beige buttercream with plastic wrap; cover remaining chocolate buttercream with plastic wrap.

## Decorating the cake

*12- by 24-inch cardboard base, double thickness, covered with parchment*

**1.** Decorate the bat's face before assembling the cake. Frost head portion with chocolate buttercream, spreading it as smoothly as possible.

**2.** Using an outline-and-fill-in technique, pipe eyes with tube 6 lime green. Smooth eyes with a small spatula dipped in hot water and dried. Wash and dry tube 6.

**3.** Pipe pupils of eyes with tube 2 chocolate. Wash and dry tube 2, then attach it to a decorating bag and fill with the ¼ cup of white buttercream. Pipe a tube 2 white dot to accent the pupil of each eye. Wash and dry tube 2.

**4.** Using a pull and push motion, pipe a tube 4 lavender nose, about the size of a jelly bean. Wash and dry tube 4.

**5.** Attach tube 4 to a decorating bag; fill with orange buttercream. Pipe smiling mouth. Attach tube 2 to bag of orange; pipe cheek lines at each end of mouth. Outline upper part of ears and feet.

**6.** Attach tube 13 to bag of white; pipe two small curved shells to resemble fangs. Wash and dry tube 13.

**7.** Insert tube 13 into a parchment cone; fill with beige buttercream. Pipe ear and feet areas with tube 13 stars.

**8.** Transfer body to cardboard base. Position wings on body, securing with a bit of chocolate buttercream. Spread chocolate over seams to level and fill in any gaps. Pipe tube 4 orange lines for wings and tail.

**9.** Attach tube 17 to bag of chocolate. Outline bat's face with stars, piping a widow's peak between his ears. Pipe stars to completely cover sides of cake, then fill in wing and body to complete decoration.

# Della Robbia Wreath

Celebrate Thanksgiving with this spectacular bounty of marzipan fruits crowning a Vanilla Brandy-Yogurt Cake. Or, decorate it for the Christmas season, using a White Velvet Fruitcake baked in a 10-inch tube pan and ivory-colored buttercream. The marzipan fruits are time-consuming to prepare, but they can easily be made a few days in advance. Here is a good chance to share a fun event with your family by enlisting their aid to make cherries and grapes.

## Preparing the marzipan or mock marzipan

*2 recipes Marzipan or Mock Marzipan (see note)*

*Paste food colors: lemon yellow, orange, moss green, pink, malt brown, violet, navy or royal blue, red*

*Liquid food color: red*

*¼ cup (approximately) vodka, light rum or kirsch*

*Whole cloves*

*1 egg white, lightly beaten*

*Special equipment: food grater, artist's brush, 10-inch tube*

Note: Because marzipan requires extensive kneading, it is easier to make one batch at a time. With the exception of the grapes, the fruits can be prepared up to a week in advance. Allow at least 24 hours, but no more than 48 hours advance for the grapes, to allow time for the assembled bunches to set. The individual grapes are attached to each other with egg white which will hold them in place for several days, but with time, the egg white will dry out, and the grapes eventually fall off. Keep main portion of marzipan dough covered with plastic wrap as you work.

**1.** For bananas, pull off enough dough to form a ball about 2 inches in diameter; tint it yellow. Divide and roll the dough between the palms of your hands into eight smaller balls of equal size. Roll each ball into an elongated banana shape with slightly pinched ends. Curve bananas slightly; place on a tray lined with waxed paper. Dip an artist's brush into brown food color, and paint markings on bananas.

**2.** For oranges, pull off enough dough to form a ball about 2 inches in diameter; tint it orange. Divide and roll dough into five smaller balls of equal size. Roll each ball over a food grater to give it texture. Insert a whole clove into the top of each orange; transfer to tray.

**3.** For pears, pull off enough dough to form a ball about 2 inches in diameter; tint pale green. Divide and roll dough into 6 smaller balls of equal size. Shape each ball into a pear by pulling one end and working it with your fingers. Insert clove stems. Pour a teaspoon of vodka onto a saucer; stir in a bit of yellow food color. Paint a yellow blush on each pear. Transfer to tray.

**4.** For apricots, pull off enough dough to form a ball about 2 inches in diameter. Using a small amount of pink and yellow food colors, tint dough a very pale apricot color. Divide and roll dough into seven smaller balls of equal size. Shape each ball into a rounded oval. Using the dull edge of a dinner knife, press a groove along the uppermost side of each apricot. Insert clove stems. Pour a teaspoon of vodka onto a saucer; stir in pink food color. Paint pink blush on each apricot. Transfer to tray.

**5.** For plums, pull off enough dough to form a ball about 1¾ inches in diameter; tint pink. Divide and roll into 5 smaller balls of equal size. Shape each into a rounded oval. Using the dull edge of a dinner knife, press a groove along the uppermost side of each plum. Insert clove stems. Pour a teaspoon of vodka onto a saucer; tint to deep violet. Paint entire surface of plums and place on a rack to dry. Transfer to tray later.

**6.** For cherries, tint remaining dough pink. Pull off a small piece of pink dough and roll it into a ball about ⅝ inch in diameter. Make about 35 balls. Combine 1 tablespoon vodka with 1 teaspoon red liquid food coloring. Paint the surface of each cherry bright red; dry on rack. Transfer to tray later.

**7.** Store remaining pink dough in an air-tight container in the refrigerator until you are ready to make the grapes. Allow dough to come to room temperature. Using blue and a bit of red, tint dough a grape color. The grape bunches are shaped and dried on the outside of a 10-inch tube pan. Spray the top and upper sides of the pan with a non-stick coating. Pull

off enough dough to form a ball about ¾ inch in diameter. To make a base for the bunch of grapes, shape ball into a pear, then flatten it slightly. Drape this shape over the edge of the pan with the widest part on top of the pan and the narrow end hanging over the edge. Press lightly to secure. To make grapes, roll about 40 balls varying in size from ¼ inch to ⅜ inch in diameter. Attach grapes to the base, one at a time, using a brush dipped in egg white as a sticking agent. Surround the outside edges of the base with grapes first; fill in the center, then stick remaining grapes on top of first layer to round out the bunch. Repeat procedure, making five bunches in all. Air-dry on pan at least 24 hours. To remove bunches from pan, carefully slide a small spatula from behind the top of each bunch, pushing it forward until loose. Lift off each bunch, and place it on the edge of another pan so that you can use the 10-inch tube pan to bake your cake.

## Preparing the cake

*Turntable*

*1 10-inch tube cake, cooled to room temperature and leveled*

*1 recipe Jam Glaze*

*10-inch round cardboard base, covered with parchment*

**1.** Level cake and transfer to a rack; brush on warm jam glaze, then let stand for about an hour to set.

**2.** Transfer cake to prepared cardboard base using a bit of glaze or buttercream to secure it in place. Place on a turntable to decorate.

## Preparing the frosting

*½ recipe Classic Buttercream*

*Paste food colors: green, blue, pink, lemon yellow*

*Tubes: 30, 67 (optional)*

*2 parchment cones*

Mix and tint buttercream the day before or while waiting for the glaze to set.

**1.** Using green and just a touch of blue, tint ½ cup buttercream a mossy green color. Transfer to a parchment cone cut into the shape of a small leaf tube or fitted with tube 67.

**2.** Using pink and yellow, tint remaining buttercream a pale peach color. Fit a parchment cone with tube 30; fill with peach. Cover remaining buttercream with plastic wrap.

## Decorating the cake

*Decorating comb*

*½ cup (approximately) light corn syrup, warmed*

**1.** Using bowl of peach buttercream, begin by frosting part way down center hole of cake. Use a long, hot spatula to smooth the frosting as best you can.

**2.** Spread peach buttercream evenly over top of cake, but don't worry about smoothing it too much, since it will be almost completely covered with fruits.

**3.** Frost side of cake as evenly as possible. (Do not use a hot spatula.) To make grooved pattern, hold the teeth of the decorating comb at a right angle to the cake and lightly touching. Rotate the turntable without moving the comb; stop rotation when you return to the starting point. Remove comb. Transfer cake to serving platter.

**4.** Pipe tube 30 shell border around base of cake with bag of peach.

**5.** Measure and mark position of grape bunches at top edge of cake. Carefully transfer grape bunches to cake. Arrange remaining fruits on top of cake. Glaze fruits using an artist's brush dipped into warmed corn syrup.

**6.** Pipe green leaves under and in between fruits.

**7.** To serve cake, remove fruits from portion of cake that you wish to slice. Cut cake; transfer to plates and garnish each slice with some fruit.

# Bûche de Noël

The *bûche de Noël*, or yule log, is one of the most charming of traditional French holiday cakes, and it warms many a hearth the world over on Christmas eve. Made from a chocolate cake roll filled and frosted with buttercream, it is decorated with glazed-marzipan holly leaves and berries. Only a small amount of marzipan is needed. If you don't have any on hand, make a full recipe and store what you don't use in the freezer. Decorate the same cake for Washington's Birthday, substituting oval leaves and cherries made from marzipan.

## Preparing the marzipan or mock marzipan

*1 recipe Marzipan or Mock Marzipan*
*Paste food colors: super Christmas red, green*

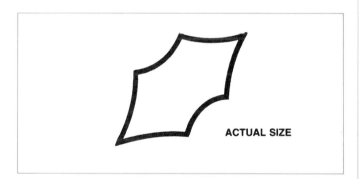

ACTUAL SIZE

**1.** Trace holly leaf (above) onto a sheet of paper; cut out pattern.

**2.** Tint about ½ cup marzipan bright green. To make holly, roll marzipan ⅛ inch thick between two sheets of plastic wrap generously sprinkled with confectioners' sugar. Carefully peel off top sheet of paper; brush excess sugar away with a pastry brush. Run a long spatula underneath the marzipan to make sure it hasn't stuck. Using a sharp knife, cut around pattern and make at least six leaves. Drape leaves over a rolling pin sprinkled with confectioners' sugar. Press a dull-edged knife into the surface of each leaf to form the veins. Air-dry on the rolling pin several hours to give them a curved shape.

**3.** Tint about 2 tablespoons marzipan red. Roll into balls, about ¼-inch in diameter to form berries. Air-dry on a sheet of waxed paper.

## Preparing the cake

*1 11- by 17-inch Chocolate Cake Roll, freshly baked, cooled and still wrapped in a towel*
*1 recipe Classic Buttercream*

**1.** Mix buttercream while cake is cooling.

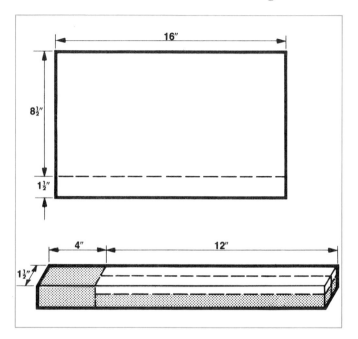

**2.** Carefully unroll cake, but do not force it flat. Measure and cut off a lengthways strip (see diagram) 1½-inch wide. Set strip aside; it will be used to form the knots on the log.

**3.** Spread white buttercream, about ⅜-inch thick, over the unrolled cake. Reroll, using the towel underneath to help lift the cake. Discard towel. Place cake seam side down on a serving platter. Set aside.

**4.** To make cake roll knots, cut 4-inches in length off the cake strip; discard. Cut the long strip in half lengthways, to make two narrower strips. Slice a thin layer off the top of each strip to reduce its thickness slightly. Spread each strip with white buttercream; reroll. Remove excess buttercream with a small spatula. Allow buttercream to crystalize slightly, then press it flat with a sheet of plastic wrap. Remove stray cake crumbs with a tweezer. Cover knots with plastic wrap and set aside.

## Preparing the frosting

*⅔ cup unsweetened cocoa*

*3 tablespoons butter*

*⅛ teaspoon salt*

*Several teaspoons milk*

*1 tablespoon piping gel, plain or red*

*Paste food colors: super Christmas red*

*Tube: 2*

*1 parchment cone*

**1.** Place ¼ cup white buttercream and 1 tablespoon piping gel into a small mixing bowl; stir to mix. Tint red. Transfer to paper cone fitted with tube 2; set aside.

**2.** Add cocoa, butter, salt, and two teaspoons milk to the remaining white buttercream (about half the recipe). Beat until fluffy and smooth, adding more milk to thin, if necessary. Cover with plastic wrap.

## Decorating the cake

*Light corn syrup*

**1.** Arrange strips of waxed paper around the cake to keep the serving platter clean.

**2.** Spread cake with chocolate buttercream, running the spatula back and forth for a rough-bark surface texture.

**3.** Arrange knots on top of cake; frost sides.

**4.** Write or print the word "Noel" with the cone of red.

**5.** Arrange holly and berries on cake. Brush with warmed corn syrup to glaze.

**6.** Protect exposed cake surfaces with plastic wrap until serving time. Remove waxed paper from around cake.

# Champagne Bottle Cake

Toast the New Year with a mouth-watering cake decorated to look like a magnum of pink Champagne. A mixture of buttercream and piping gel adds luster to the cake's surface and provides a smooth, satiny background on which to place the stylized royal-icing flowers.

Because many of my friends are wine buffs, I have also used this bottle-shaped cake as a birthday surprise, decorated to resemble a great old wine or a favorite wine. Simply change the color scheme and duplicate the appropriate wine label and other bottle details in piped buttercream. A word of caution: avoid decorating green-colored wine bottles; dark green frosting tastes bitter and stains the mouth. White wines, such as Burgundies and Sauternes, that come in clear bottles work well, as do rosé wines or Rhine wines which come in brown bottles (mocha frosting).

## Preparing the decorations

*1 recipe Royal Icing, stiffened*

*Tube: 61*

*Flower nail*

At least six hours in advance, pipe several tube 61, white, stylized, royal-icing flowers of various shapes and sizes. The flowers are best formed on a flower nail. Air-dry on a cookie sheet.

## Preparing the cake

*1 9- by 13-inch cake layer, cooled to room temperature and leveled*

*1 recipe Jam Glaze*

*5½- by 14-inch cardboard base, double-thickness, cut to shape of bottle and covered with parchment*

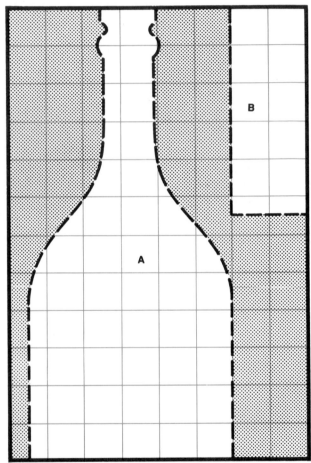

**EACH SQUARE EQUALS 1 INCH**
**CUT OFF AND DISCARD GRAY AREAS**

Note that a cake baked in a 9- by 13-inch pan measures about 8 by 12 inches when turned out.

**1.** Using diagram as a guide, draw pattern of bottle onto parchment or waxed paper; cut out pattern.

**2.** Place pattern on cake; cut out cake sections. Using a sharp knife, slightly bevel the top edge of the cake sections.

**3.** Transfer cake sections to rack. Brush on warm jam glaze, then air-dry for about an hour, until set.

107

**4.** Using paper pattern, prepare cardboard base and cover with parchment. Position cake sections on cardboard base, using a bit of glaze or buttercream to secure in place.

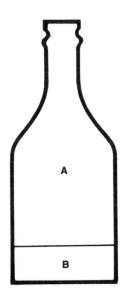

## Preparing the frosting

*1 recipe Classic Buttercream*

*Clear piping gel*

*Paste food colors: copper, burgundy, mint green, lemon yellow*

*Tubes: 1, 2, 6, 65s, 66*

*1 decorating bag, fitted with a coupling*

*4 parchment cones*

Mix and tint buttercream the day before or while waiting for glaze to set.

**1.** Tint ¼ cup buttercream yellow; cover with plastic wrap.

**2.** Tint ½ cup buttercream mint green; transfer to decorating bag fitted with tube 2.

**3.** Tint remaining buttercream pale copper. Divide pale copper between two bowls; cover one bowl with plastic wrap and set aside. Darken tint of other bowl to a medium shade of copper; remove ¼ cup of medium copper and cover remaining medium copper with plastic wrap. Using additional copper coloring with a bit of burgundy, tint the ¼ cup of medium copper a darker reddish copper shade. Cover with plastic wrap.

**4.** Set aside remaining tubes and cones.

## Decorating the cake

**1.** Frost neck of bottle with a layer of medium copper buttercream, spreading it as smoothly as possible. Add an equal amount of piping gel to the remaining medium copper buttercream; spread mixture smoothly over pre-frosted neck of bottle. Using a knife, remove excess frosting at the point between the neck and shoulder of the bottle, leaving a neat, straight line. Place remaining medium copper buttercream-gel mixture into a parchment cone fitted with tube 6; set aside.

**2.** Frost bottle area of cake with a layer of pale copper buttercream. Add an equal amount of piping gel to the remaining pale copper buttercream; spread mixture smoothly over the pre-frosted bottle area of cake. Set aside remaining pale copper buttercream-gel mixture, covered with plastic wrap.

**3.** Arrange royal icing flowers on cake. Pipe tube 2 green stems and message. Attach tube 65s to bag of green; pipe small leaves. Attach tube 66 to bag of green; pipe larger leaves at bottom corner of bottle. Attach tube 1 to bag of green; pipe a few green stamens in center of two largest flowers.

**4.** Wash and dry tube 1; insert in a parchment cone; fill with yellow buttercream. Pipe a few dots in center of two largest flowers.

**5.** Wash and dry tube 2; insert in a parchment cone; fill with reddish copper. Pipe lines and dots to decorate neck of bottle.

**6.** Transfer cake to serving platter of your choice. Using tube 6 medium copper, pipe a caulking line around neck of bottle.

**7.** Wash and dry tube 6; insert into a parchment cone; fill with pale copper. Pipe a caulking line around base of bottle.

# Sporty Cakes

# Blue Ribbon Cake

**Life is full of contests, and you'll probably think of many occasions to decorate this blue ribbon cake. Use it to celebrate club or school elections, scholastic achievements, job promotions, as well as sporting events. Practice ruffles on an inverted cake pan, and be sure to use a jam glaze which will serve the purpose of strengthening the ribbon tails before frosting.**

## Preparing the cake

*1 8-inch square cake layer, cooled to room temperature and leveled*

*1 9-inch round cake layer, cooled to room temperature and leveled*

*1 recipe Jam Glaze*

Note that a cake baked in an 8-inch square pan measures about 7 inches square when turned out.

**1.** Slice two 2- by 7-inch strips from the square layer. Cut points at one end of each strip; cut a curve at the opposite end so that the ribbon tails will fit snugly against the round layer when the cake is assembled.

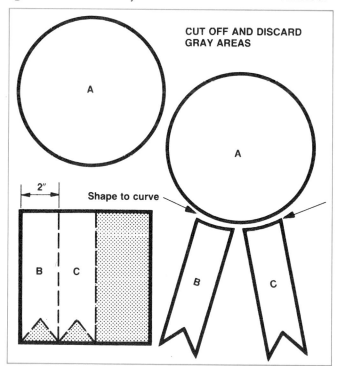

**2.** Transfer cake sections to a rack; brush on warm jam glaze and allow to set for about an hour.

## Preparing the frosting

*1 recipe Classic Buttercream*

*Paste food colors: royal or navy blue, red, lemon yellow*

Mix and tint buttercream while waiting for glaze to set.

**1.** Tint about 1 cup buttercream lemon yellow. Transfer it to a decorating bag fitted with tube 2.

**2.** Using royal or navy blue and just a tiny bit of red, tint about half the remaining buttercream a medium shade of blue. Cover with plastic.

**3.** Set aside about 1 cup white buttercream; cover with plastic wrap.

**4.** Tint remaining buttercream light blue by stirring in a small amount of the medium-blue buttercream. Cover with plastic wrap.

## Decorating the cake

*Tubes: 2, 4, 20, 125*

*2 decorating bags, fitted with couplings*

*1 parchment cone*

*12- by 20-inch cardboard base, double thickness, covered with parchment*

**1.** Transfer round layer to a turntable. Spread white buttercream as smoothly as possible over the center of the round layer, covering an area about 6-inches in diameter. (You don't have to spread it all the way to the edge, because ruffles will cover that portion of the cake.) Use a toothpick, poking small holes in the white frosting, to mark a 5-inch circle in the middle of the cake.

**2.** Frost sides of round layer medium blue.

**3.** To make two-tone ruffles, fill one side of a decorating bag with light blue, the other side with medium blue. Attach tube 125, aligning the wide tip of

the tube with the light blue. Beginning at the edge, pipe a ruffled layer around the cake with the wide tip of the tube pointing outward and the narrow tip pointing toward the center. Refill bag, if necessary. Pipe a second ruffled layer in front of and slightly overlapping the first. Repeat procedure for the third layer, bringing ruffle to the edge of, but not entering the 5-inch white circle.

**4.** Pipe tube 2 yellow message within white circle. Attach tube 20 to bag of yellow; pipe ribbed line around perimeter of white circle. Transfer round layer to prepared cardboard base.

**5.** Working on one ribbon tail at a time, transfer to turntable, frost top and sides medium blue.

**6.** Attach tube 2 to bag of yellow; pipe name and year on tails. Transfer to base, fitting tails to round layer.

**7.** Insert tube 4 into a parchment cone; fill with medium blue. Pipe a caulking line around base of cake and tail seams.

# Tennis Racquet Cake

Tennis players will have a ball with this cake, especially since it is practically life-size. A miniature table tennis board makes an ideal serving platter, but a 12- by 30-inch cardboard base covered with parchment works equally well. If you do use a table tennis board, then you will need a 10- by 28-inch piece of cardboard, cut to the exact shape of the racquet and covered with parchment, on which to place the cake. The tennis balls are baked in greased and floured, metal egg-poaching cups because they have rounded bottoms. Place a few tablespoons of water into each of the empty cavities of a cupcake pan, and set the poaching cups over the cavities, which will hold them level while baking. Alternatively, you can cut the balls from pieces of scrap cake with a round biscuit cutter.

## Preparing the cake

*11- by 17- by 1-inch sheet cake, cooled to room temperature and leveled*

*3 cupcakes, baked in metal egg-poaching cups (optional)*

*1 recipe Jam Glaze*

Note that a cake baked in an 11- by 17-inch pan measures about 10 by 16 inches when turned out.

**1.** Make a pattern for the racquet head and cut cake as illustrated. Cut three circular shapes for balls from scraps, if necessary.

**2.** Place cake sections and balls on a rack. Brush on warm jam glaze; air-dry for about an hour, until set.

## Preparing the frosting

*1 recipe Classic Buttercream*

*3 tablespoons unsweetened cocoa*

*1 tablespoon butter, softened*

*2 teaspoons (approximately) milk*

*Paste food colors: lemon yellow, navy or royal blue*

*Tubes: 2, 3, 4, 6, 67*

*2 decorating bags, fitted with couplings*

*2 parchment cones*

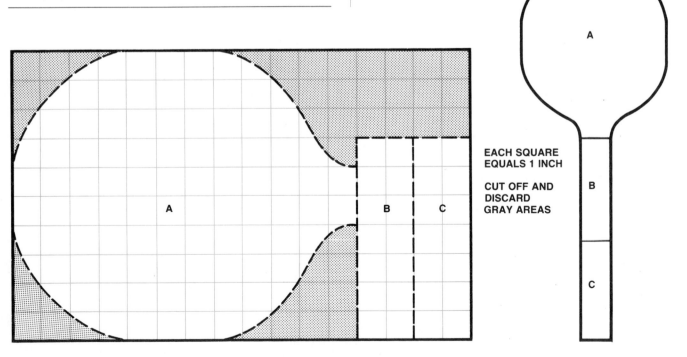

EACH SQUARE
EQUALS 1 INCH

CUT OFF AND
DISCARD
GRAY AREAS

Mix and tint buttercream the day before or while waiting for glaze to set.

1. Tint 1 cup buttercream lemon yellow. Place ¼ cup yellow into a parchment cone fitted with tube 2. Cover remaining yellow with plastic wrap.

2. Tint ½ cup buttercream blue. Transfer to decorating bag fitted with tube 3.

3. Place 1 cup buttercream into a bowl; add cocoa and butter, stirring to mix. Adding one teaspoon of milk at a time, thin buttercream to spreading consistency. Transfer to decorating bag fitted with tube 4.

4. Cover remaining white buttercream with plastic wrap.

## Decorating the cake

*12- by 30-inch cardboard base, double thickness, and covered with parchment*

1. Place racquet-head section of cake on a turntable. Frost top and sides white.

2. Mark outline for strings with toothpick punctures; with tube 2, pipe yellow strings.

3. Pipe tube 4 chocolate line around perimeter of strings. Transfer racquet head to prepared cardboard base.

4. Attach handle sections to head using frosting to hold them in place. Frost top and sides of handle white, using a hot spatula to smooth the seams.

5. Print message with tube 4 chocolate.

6. Decorate neck grip by piping a series of diagonal lines—two lines with tube 4 chocolate, one line tube 3 blue and so on.

7. Attach tube 6 to bag of chocolate. Pipe top and base outline of racquet, by-passing the neck grip at the top edge.

8. Pipe tube 3 stretch bands in blue around racquet frame. Change to tube 67. Pipe blue ruffles in a series of diagonal lines to represent handle grip.

9. Decorate cupcakes on a number 14 flower nail or on top of a jar. Frost cupcakes lemon yellow. Wash and dry tube 2; insert into a parchment cone; fill with white. Pipe curved lines on balls. Transfer balls to serving board.

# Football Cake

Win or lose, you will add to the excitement of the day with this scrumptious chocolate football cake. Serve it at a tailgate picnic when the whole gang goes out to the stadium—or the peewee-league field. If everyone is gathered around the television watching the game, you can escape to the peaceful solitude of the kitchen to decorate the cake for after the game; it's that quick and easy to make. Or serve it to a group of neighborhood football widows to celebrate the end of the ever-expanding season.

You need a special egg-shaped pan for this three-dimensional cake. If you don't have one, you could bake a high, rounded 9-inch square cake layer and then carve off and discard two opposite corners to get a good facsimile of a football.

## Preparing the cake

*2 cake layers baked in an egg-shaped pan, cooled to room temperature*

*1 recipe Jam Glaze*

**1.** Level cake layers so that they will fit together. Cut a slice from under the bottom layer so that the cake will stand straight when assembled.

**2.** Place cake layers on a rack; brush warm jam glaze over the outside of the cakes, then air-dry for about an hour, until set.

**3.** Transfer bottom cake layer to a platter; spread a thin layer of chocolate buttercream over the top and sides.

**4.** Position top layer. Spread a thin layer of chocolate buttercream over top.

## Preparing the frosting

*½ recipe Classic Buttercream*

*⅔ cup sifted unsweetened cocoa*

*3 tablespoons butter, softened*

*⅛ teaspoon salt*

*Several teaspoons milk*

*Paste food color: black*

Mix and tint buttercream the day before or while waiting for the glaze to set.

**1.** Place about ¼ cup buttercream into each of two small bowls; tint one bowl black, leave the other white. Cover each with plastic wrap.

**2.** Add cocoa, butter, salt, and 2 teaspoons milk to the mixing bowl containing the remaining buttercream.

**3.** Beat at medium speed until light and fluffy. Thin with additional teaspoons of milk, if necessary. Cover with plastic wrap.

## Decorating the cake

*Tubes: 2, 18, 46*

*1 decorating bag, fitted with coupling*

*2 parchment cones*

**1.** Fit tube 18 to the decorating bag and fill with chocolate buttercream. Pipe stars over entire surface of cake.

**2.** Insert tube 46 into a parchment cone and fill with white buttercream. Pipe two long laces, side by side, on top of the football with the serrated side of the tube upward. Pipe short laces over the long ones with the flat side of the tube upward.

**3.** Insert tube 2 into a parchment cone and fill with black buttercream. Pipe traditional black design around white laces.

# Baseball and Mitt Cake

This cake will make a home-run hit with baseball fans of any age. Since the mitt is made of just one 9-inch round cake layer, the remaining cake batter is used to bake cupcakes, decorated to look like baseballs. Notice that the ball on the mitt is rounder than the cupcake balls. It was baked in a greased and floured, metal egg-poaching cup that was placed over an empty cavity of the cupcake pan to keep it level. Using a bit of frosting to hold it in place, the ball was decorated on a number 14 flower nail. If you don't have this large nail, decorate the small, rounded cake on top of a jar or can. If you don't have a set of metal egg-poaching cups, substitute one of the cupcakes and build up the frosting for a rounder look.

## Preparing the cake

*1 9-inch round cake layer, cooled to room temperature and leveled*

*7 cupcakes, or as many as can be baked with the leftover batter*

*1 recipe Jam Glaze*

*8-inch round cardboard base, covered with parchment*

Note that a cake baked in a 9-inch round pan measures about 8 inches in diameter when turned out.

**1.** Make a pattern for the mitt by tracing an 8-inch circle onto a sheet of parchment or waxed paper; cut out circle. Using the photograph as a guide, draw outline of thumb and fingers on the circle.

**2.** Place round layer and one cupcake (with the paper liner peeled off) onto a rack. Brush on warm jam glaze; air-dry for about an hour, until set.

**3.** Transfer cake to cardboard base, using a bit of glaze or buttercream to secure it. Place pattern atop cake, and, using a toothpick to poke holes through the pattern, mark outline of thumb and fingers.

## Preparing the frosting

*1 recipe Classic Buttercream*

*3 tablespoons unsweetened cocoa*

*1 tablespoon butter, softened*

*2 teaspoons (approximately) milk*

*Paste food colors: super Christmas red, egg yellow, malt brown*

*Tubes 2, 4, 6, 18*

*2 decorating bags, fitted with couplings*

*1 parchment cone*

Mix and tint buttercream the day before or while waiting for glaze to set.

**1.** Tint ¼ cup buttercream red; cover with plastic.

**2.** Place 1 cup buttercream into a bowl; stir in cocoa and butter. Adding one teaspoon of milk at a time, thin buttercream to a spreading consistency. Transfer to a decorating bag fitted with tube 4.

**3.** Place 1½ cups white buttercream into a bowl; cover with plastic wrap.

**4.** Using egg yellow and malt brown, tint remaining buttercream tan. Attach tube 18 to a decorating bag; fill with tan. Cover remaining tan with plastic wrap.

## Decorating the cake

**1.** Spread a layer of smooth, tan frosting on top of the cake just to cover the area between the thumb and forefinger.

**2.** Outline mitt (including thumb and fingers) with tube 4 chocolate.

**3.** Pipe tube 18 tan stars to completely cover side of cake. Pipe tube 18 tan stars within the outline of the mitt area.

**4.** Attach tube 6 to bag of tan. Pipe a line around the edge of the cake between the thumb and forefinger.

**5.** Attach tube 2 to bag of chocolate. Pipe stitching on smooth tan area between thumb and forefinger. Change back to tube 4, pipe detailed stitching on mitt area and on top of the tan line between the thumb and forefinger.

**6.** Frost glazed cupcake and tops of remaining cupcakes white.

**7.** Wash and dry tube 2; insert into a parchment cone and fill with red. Pipe stitching on baseballs, making sure to reverse the direction of the arrow stitching on each side of the ball. Position baseball on top of mitt. Arrange cupcakes around mitt.

# Sailboat

Personalize this colorful sailboat by printing a name on its hull. For a birthday, insert the appropriate number of candles in a line alongside the mast, and number the top of the jib (smaller sail) with the age of the person or date of the celebration. Because the sailboat sections are placed so near to each other when the cake is assembled, it's easier to decorate each section prior to positioning it on a cakeboard or serving platter. To transport cake for a picnic, arrange decorated sections in their original square layout, but leave a space between so that the pieces don't touch. Don't forget to take along a parchment-covered cakeboard or other serving platter. The cake can be transported in a square box, and assembled on the board once you arrive at your destination.

## Preparing the cake

*1 9-inch square cake layer, cooled to room temperature and leveled*

*1 recipe Jam Glaze*

Note that a cake baked in a 9-inch square pan, measures about 8-inches square when turned out.

**1.** Cut cake into three sections as shown in diagram.

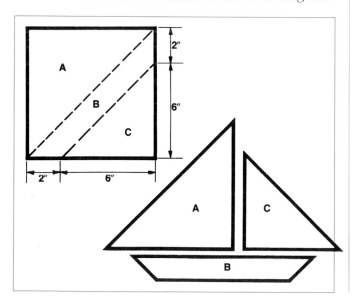

**2.** Place sections on a rack; brush on warm jam glaze, then air-dry for about an hour, until set.

## Preparing the frosting

*1 recipe Classic Buttercream*

*Paste food colors: sky blue, green, pink, orange, lemon yellow*

*Tubes: 8, 22, 48*

*1 decorating bag, fitted with a coupling*

*5 parchment cones*

Mix and tint buttercream the day before or while waiting for glaze to set.

**1.** Tint 1 cup buttercream blue; place in a decorating bag fitted with tube 48.

**2.** Place ½ cup buttercream into each of four small bowls; tint bowls green, pink, orange and yellow. Cover each bowl with plastic wrap.

**3.** Place ¼ cup white buttercream into a parchment cone fitted with tube 8. Cover remaining white buttercream with plastic wrap.

## Decorating the cake

*12- by 16-inch cardboard base, double thickness, covered with parchment.*

**1.** Frost sides of main sail white; frost sides and top of hull and jib sail white. Use a hot spatula to smooth.

**2.** Divide and mark main sail into five bands, allowing a slightly wider band for the yellow portion at the top of the sail. Beginning at the bottom, mast side of the main sail, pipe blue area with tube 48, serrated-side up.

**3.** Wash and dry tube 48; insert into a parchment cone; fill with green. Pipe green area on main sail. Repeat procedure with pink, orange and yellow.

**4.** Trim excess colored frosting from wide end of main sail with a sharp knife. Pipe tube 8 white mast.

**5.** Attach tube 22 to bag of blue; pipe scroll waves on hull. Transfer decorated sections to cardboard base or serving platter.

# Athletic Shoe Cakes

Anyone, child or adult, who's attached to their athletic shoes will jump for joy when they're presented with this pair of cakes. You might even like to pipe a message or greeting in the white area of one shoe and the person's name in the other. The pair is cut from one cake layer, baked in a 9- by 13- by 2-inch pan, and is quite easy to assemble. If you decide to change the color scheme, remember that the cake will taste better if decorated in pastels. Dark colors, if used, should be limited to the striped area of the shoes as a color accent only.

## Preparing the cake

1 9- by 13-inch cake layer, cooled to room temperature

1 recipe Jam Glaze

2 4- by 8-inch cardboard cake bases

Parchment paper

Note that a cake baked in a 9- by 13-inch pan measures about 8- by 12-inches when turned out.

**1.** Level cake to a height of 1¼ inches.

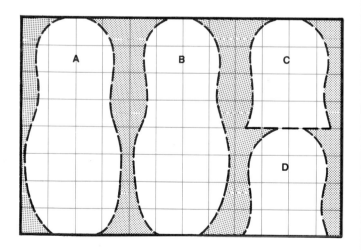

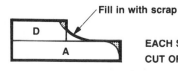

Fill in with scrap

**EACH SQUARE EQUALS 1 INCH**
**CUT OFF AND DISCARD GRAY AREAS**

**2.** Using diagram as a guide, draw a pattern for one shoe on a 4- by 8-inch piece of paper; cut out pattern.

**3.** Cut cake into two 4- by 8-inch pieces and two 4 by 4-inch pieces as shown in diagram. Place paper shoe pattern onto one of the 4- by 8-inch cakes; cut cake in shape of shoe. *Reverse paper pattern* and place on remaining 4- by 8-inch cake; cut cake in shape of opposite shoe. Repeat procedure for heel portions, remembering to reverse the pattern when cutting the second heel.

**4.** Assemble cakes; cut out pieces of the end scraps to fill in area as indicated in diagram. If necessary, shave small pieces off the asembled cakes, using a sharp knife to carve the desired shape.

**5.** Disassemble cakes, placing cut-out cake pieces onto a rack; brush on warm jam glaze.

**6.** Using paper pattern, trace right and left shoes onto cardboard; cut out, then line cardboard shoe shapes with parchment.

**7.** Reassemble glazed cake pieces on top of cardboard bases. The jam should still be tacky enough to hold the pieces in place, but if desired, you may also spread a thin layer of buttercream between the pieces. Let assembled cakes air-dry for about an hour, until set.

## Preparing the frosting

1 recipe Classic Buttercream

Paste food colors: orange, green, yellow

Tubes: 6, 17

3 decorating bags, fitted with couplings

2 parchment cones

Mix and tint buttercream while waiting for glazed cakes to set.

**1.** Tint about 1¾ cups buttercream a medium shade of orange, transfer to decorating bag fitted with tube 6.

**2.** Tint about 1¾ cups buttercream pale orange; cover with plastic wrap.

**3.** Place ¼ cup buttercream into each of two bowls. Tint green and yellow. Transfer green to a parch-

ment cone fitted with tube 17; cover bowl of yellow with plastic wrap.

**4.** Cover remaining white buttercream with plastic wrap.

**5.** Set aside remaining equipment.

## Decorating the cake

**1.** Using the photograph as a guide, frost tongue area and opening of both shoes with a smooth layer of white buttercream.

**2.** Pipe tube 6, medium-orange lines where indicated in the photographs.

**3.** Pipe two rows of tube 17 green stars to form stripes on both sides of each shoe. Wash and dry tube 17; place in a parchment cone and fill with yellow. Pipe one row of tube 17 yellow stars in front of each green stripe.

**4.** Wash and dry tube 17; attach to a decorating bag and fill with pale orange. Pipe stars in areas indicated in the photograph.

**5.** Wash and dry tube 17; attach to bag of medium orange. Pipe stars in areas indicated in the photograph.

**6.** Wash and dry tube 17; attach to a decorating bag and fill with white. Pipe stars around base of shoes, beginning with two rows in the back and tapering down to one row as you near the front of the shoes.

**7.** Wash and dry tube 6; attach to bag of white. Pipe laces.

# Cowboy Boot

Hey, partner! Rodeo fans and country-and-western music lovers should get a kick out of this cake. Decorate it for a square dance, a western style cook-out, or a birthday. The butterfly wings and teardrop-shaped decorations are made with semisweet chocolate. Notice the attractive tweed-like speckles in the gold-colored frosting. This happens when paste food color is added to the buttercream in a large blob, all at once, instead of being mixed in slowly, a little at a time. The coloring doesn't have a chance to dissolve completely, and the buttercream takes on a flecked appearance.

## Preparing the cake

*1 9- by 13-inch cake layer, cooled to room temperature and leveled*

*1 recipe Jam Glaze*

*10 by 14-inch cardboard base, double thickness*

*Parchment paper*

Note that a cake baked in a 9- by 13-inch pan measures about 8 by 12 inches when turned out.

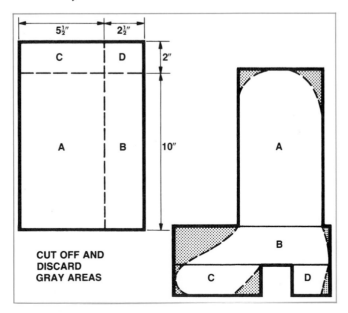

1. Cut cake into four sections; assemble as shown in diagram, and make additional cuts to form the shape of a boot.

2. Place boot sections on one cardboard base; trace boot pattern onto base.

3. Transfer boot sections to a rack. Brush on warm jam glaze and let stand for about an hour or until set.

4. Cut boot shape out of both pieces of cardboard; tape sections together, then cover with parchment. Transfer glazed cake sections to prepared base, using buttercream to hold sections in place.

## Preparing the frosting

*1 recipe Classic Buttercream*

*3 tablespoons unsweetened cocoa*

*1 tablespoon butter, softened*

*2 teaspoons (approximately) milk*

*Paste food colors: super Christmas red, egg yellow, malt brown*

*Tubes: 2, 4, 48*

*1 decorating bag, fitted with a coupling*

*3 parchment cones*

Mix and tint buttercream while waiting for glaze to set.

1. Tint ¼ cup buttercream red; cover with plastic wrap.

2. Place 1 cup buttercream into a bowl; add cocoa and butter, stirring to mix. Adding one teaspoon of milk at a time, thin buttercream to a spreading consistency. Cover with plastic wrap.

3. Add about ¼ teaspoon egg yellow and ⅛ teaspoon malt brown food coloring to the remaining buttercream. Stir to mix, adding more yellow or brown as needed to produce a golden color. Cover with plastic wrap.

4. Place ⅔ cup of golden buttercream and ⅓ cup chocolate buttercream into a small bowl. Mix thor-

**ACTUAL SIZE**

oughly to make a tan colored buttercream. Cover with plastic wrap.

**5.** Set aside remaining equipment.

## Preparing the decorations

*1 ounce semisweet chocolate*

*½ teaspoon butter*

**1.** Using a pencil, outline butterfly wings and teardrop-shaped patterns onto a sheet of waxed paper, then turn paper over and outline wings and teardrop patterns in reverse. Do not cut out. Place paper on a baking sheet for support.

**2.** Melt semisweet chocolate and ½ teaspoon butter over hot water in top of double boiler. Place in parchment cone with just a pinhole opening. (This is easy to do if you place the parchment cone into a coffee mug to hold it in place while transferring the melted chocolate mixture. The cup will also catch any chocolate that drips from the tip of the cone.)

**3.** Carefully trace outlines of wings with chocolate, then fill in. Use a small artist's brush to smooth the chocolate before it sets. Repeat procedure for teardrops. Transfer waxed paper and baking sheet to refrigerator; chill decorations until firm. They should

be ready by the time you have finished frosting the cake.

## Decorating the cake

**1.** Frost the top and sides of the boot with gold, spreading it as smoothly as possible.

**2.** Frost the sole and bottom of the heel with tan. Insert tube 48 into a parchment cone; fill with remaining tan buttercream. With serrated-side up, pipe a continuous band from the inside of the heel, over the top, then down the other side. Repeat procedure to completely cover heel.

**3.** Attach tube 2 to a decorating bag; fill with chocolate buttercream. Measure and mark the center of the boot leg. Using a long thread or a ruler mark as a guideline, pipe two straight lines on either side of the center of the boot leg, about ¾ inch apart.

**4.** Remove chocolate decorations from refrigerator. Carefully peel off the waxed paper and position decorations on cake.

**5.** Using tube 2 and chocolate buttercream, pipe remaining trim and stitches on boot. Attach tube 4 to bag of chocolate; outline boot.

**6.** Wash and dry tube 2. Insert into a parchment cone; fill with red. Pipe dots on butterfly wings.

# Children's Party Cakes

---

## A B C BLOCK

---

## PANDA

---

## POPSICLE CAKES

---

## BIRTHDAY BALLOONS CAKE

---

## SWEET 16 CAKE

---

## SLED CAKE

---

## BALLET DANCER CAKE

---

# A B C Block

Here's a darling cake that a young child or even a baby will be able to recognize. Because of their angle, the sides of the cake are a bit awkward to decorate. However, if you place the cake at eye level by setting it on a turntable and seating yourself on a low stool, the problem will be solved.

## Preparing the cake and patterns

*2 6- by 6- by 3-inch cake layers, cooled to room temperature and leveled*

*1 recipe Jam Glaze*

*6-inch square cardboard base, covered with parchment*

**1.** Place cake layers on a rack. Brush on warm jam glaze; air-dry for about an hour or until set.

**2.** Transfer one cake layer to cardboard base using a bit of glaze or buttercream to secure in place. Spread a layer of white buttercream over the top. Place second cake layer on top of frosted layer.

**3.** Trace patterns for apple and large A onto parchment or waxed paper. Cut out patterns.

## Preparing the frosting

*1 recipe Classic Buttercream*

*Paste food colors; super Christmas red, lemon yellow, leaf green, malt brown*

*Tubes: 2, 3, 4, 18, 22, 46, 66 (optional)*

*2 decorating bags, fitted with couplings*

*2 parchment cones*

Mix and tint buttercream the day before or while waiting for glaze to set.

**1.** Tint 1½ cups buttercream red; place in decorating bag fitted with tube 4.

**2.** Tint ½ cup buttercream yellow; place in decorating bag fitted with tube 3.

**3.** Tint ¼ cup buttercream green; place in a parchment cone cut into the shape of a small leaf tube or fitted with tube 66.

**4.** Tint ¼ cup buttercream brown; place in parchment cone fitted with tube 2.

**5.** Set aside remaining equipment until decorating time.

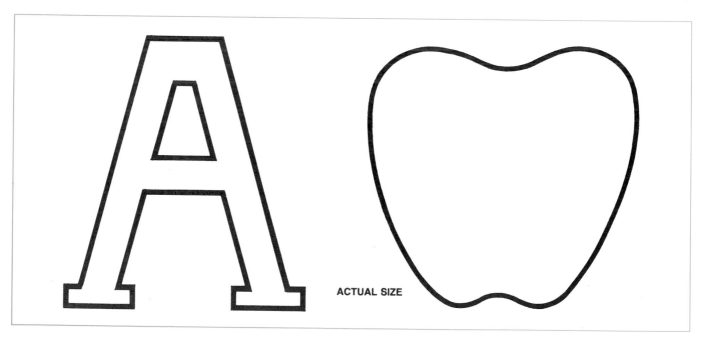

ACTUAL SIZE

## Decorating the cake

**1.** Frost top and sides of assembled cake white, spreading the buttercream as smoothly as possible.

**2.** Mark apple pattern on two opposite sides of the cake with toothpick punctures. Mark large A pattern on two opposite sides of the cake with toothpick punctures. Outline apples and A's with tube 4 red. Pipe tube 4 red capital and lower case A's at corners of cake sides.

**3.** Attach tube 22 to bag of red. Fill apples with red stars. Pipe a tube 2 brown stem. Pipe a green leaf at the base of the stem.

**4.** Fill in large A's with tube 3 yellow dots.

**5.** Wash and dry tube 2. Attach tube 2 to bag of yellow; print message.

**6.** Attach tube 46 to bag of red. With the serrated side of the tube facing up, pipe block outline on top and sides of cake.

**7.** Wash and dry tube 4; attach to bag of yellow. Pipe yellow lines in the center of the red outlines.

**8.** Attach tube 18 to bag of yellow; pipe a rosette at each corner point.

# Panda

Yum, yum . . . the irresistible expression on this panda's face leaves no doubt that he's angling for an invitation to a child's party. And, he's so easy to decorate. His eyes and ears are made with store-bought mint patties; his entire body is piped with a large star tube.

## Preparing the cake

*1 9-inch square cake layer, cooled to room temperature and leveled*

*1 8-inch round cake layer, cooled to room temperature and leveled*

*1 recipe Jam Glaze*

Note that a cake baked in a 9-inch square pan measures about 8 inches square when turned out.

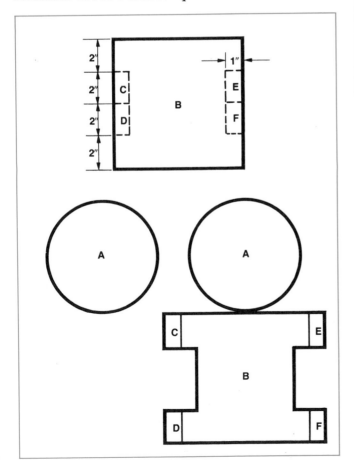

1. Cut 9-inch square layer as directed in diagram. Place all cakes pieces, including round layer, on a rack; brush on warm jam glaze. Let stand for about an hour or until set.

2. It is easier to decorate the main body (piece B) and the head (piece A) separately on a turntable prior to assembly on the cardboard base. Transfer piece B to a turntable.

## Preparing the frosting

*1 recipe Classic Buttercream, chocolate*

*½ recipe Classic Buttercream, white*

*Paste food color; super Christmas red*

*Tubes: 4, 8, 15, 16, 30*

*3 decorating bags, fitted with couplings*

Mix and tint buttercream the day before or while waiting for the glaze to set.

1. Attach tube 30 to a decorating bag and fill with chocolate buttercream. Cover remaining chocolate with plastic wrap.

2. Tint ½ cup buttercream red; transfer to decorating bag fitted with tube 4.

3. Attach tube 15 to a decorating bag and fill with white buttercream. Cover remaining white buttercream with plastic wrap.

## Decorating the cake

*18- by 24-inch cardboard base, double thickness, covered with parchment*

*4 toothpicks*

*2 large chocolate-covered mint patties*

*2 small chocolate-covered mint patties*

1. Using a toothpick, mark a 4-inch circle slightly lower center on piece B for the panda's tummy. Fill circle with tube 30 chocolate stars. Pipe chocolate stars around upper edge and sides of piece B. (Do not pipe stars at the ends of the feet where the paws will later be attached.)

2. Pipe tube 4 red outline for bow. Pipe tube 15 white stars at random within the bow tie. Attach tube 16 to bag of red, fill in bow tie with red stars.

3. Wash and dry tube 30; set aside bag of chocolate. Attach tube 30 to bag of white. Pipe stars to fill in panda's body.

4. Transfer piece B to prepared cake board. Attach paws (pieces C, D, E and F). Wash and dry tube 30; attach to bag of chocolate. Cover paws with chocolate stars. Attach tube 4 to bag of red; pipe straight lines on top of each paw for claws.

5. Transfer round cake layer to turntable. Pipe tube 30 chocolate stars around side and upper edge. Wash and dry tube 30; attach to bag of white. Pipe tube 30 white stars for panda's face.

6. Position small mint patties for panda's eyes. Attach tube 8 to bag of white. Pipe white of eyes; flatten with a hot spatula. Wash and dry tube 4; attach to bag of chocolate. Pipe pupils of eyes, button nose and curved mouth. Wash and dry tube 8; attach to bag of red. Pipe tongue.

7. Transfer head to cake board, positioning face at a slight angle. Insert two toothpicks on either side of the head, about one-third of the way down from the top, to support the ears. Cut a small slice off the edge of each large mint pattie; place patties on top of toothpick supports with cut edge toward cake.

# Popsicle Cakes

Shiny pastel popsicle cakes are as easy to make as they are to eat. They can even be used as decorations atop a larger cake for a child's birthday. Simply frost a 10- or 12-inch layer cake or a 9- by 13-inch sheet cake with white or chocolate buttercream; arrange popsicle cakes on top, allowing one popsicle for each year of the birthday child's age. Popsicle sticks can be purchased at most toy and crafts stores.

## Preparing the cake

*1 8-inch square layer, cooled to room temperature and leveled*

*½ recipe Jam Glaze*

*16 popsicle sticks*

Note that a cake baked in an 8-inch square pan measures about 7 inches square when turned out.

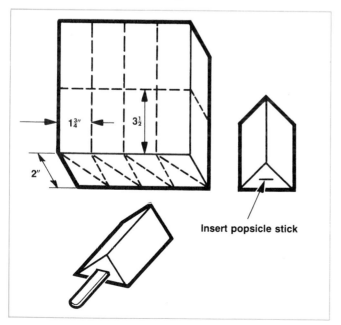

**Insert popsicle stick**

**1.** Divide cake into eight rectangles as shown in diagram. Cut each rectangle in two along the diagonal.
**2.** Place cakes on a rack and brush warm jam glaze over each. Let stand for about an hour or until set.

**3.** Insert popsicle sticks. Wrap exposed wood with aluminum foil to protect it during the frosting procedure.

## Preparing the frosting

*½ recipe Classic Buttercream (optional)*

*1 recipe Quick Fondant Icing*

*Paste food colors; pink, violet, orange, lemon yellow*

*¼ teaspoon each, strawberry, vanilla, orange, lemon extract (optional)*

Mix buttercream and prepare fondant while waiting for glaze to set. Divide fondant into four bowls; tint pink, violet, orange and yellow. Add ¼ teaspoon flavoring, strawberry, vanilla, orange, lemon to each bowl, if desired. Cover with plastic wrap.

## Decorating the cakes

**1.** Spread a smooth layer of white buttercream over the top angles of each cake. (It is not necessary to frost the ends.) This step may be omitted altogether, if desired. Some people prefer a nice creamy layer of frosting between the fondant and the cake, while others never notice if it is missing.
**2.** Place one bowl of fondant into a shallow pan filled with hot water. Stir the fondant until it becomes thin enough to pour, being careful not to let its temperature rise above 100 degrees. Arrange four cakes on a rack which has been placed over a sheet of waxed paper. Pour fondant over cakes, one at a time, smoothing it with a spatula so that it covers each cake, top angles and sides, completely. Do not coat the bottom of the cakes. Pierce any air bubbles with a straight pin as soon as they form. Scrape the drippings off the waxed paper; reheat and apply a second coat, if necessary. Repeat procedure with each color. When fondant has set, trim bottom edges of each cake with a sharp knife.
**3.** Remove foil wrapping from popsicle sticks. Arrange cakes on platter of your choice.

# Birthday Balloons Cake

The party will burst with excitement when guests spot their names piped on this special balloon birthday cake. And don't think it's for kids only. Decorate it with grown-ups' names to thank a service-organization or club committee members whose job is finally done.

Tubes 2 and 11 are repeatedly used to pipe the various colored balloons, so expect to wash and dry them many times and keep a tiny tube cleaning brush handy by the sink. The clever cake stand is made by covering the inverted cake pan with foil and then taping crepe paper around it. Because the cake itself is placed on a lined cardboard base, it doesn't come in contact with the crepe paper underneath.

## Preparing the cake

1 9- by 13-inch cake layer, cooled to room temperature and leveled

1 recipe Jam Glaze

9- by 13-inch cardboard base, covered with parchment

1. Place cake on a rack; brush on warm glaze, then air-dry for about an hour or until set.
2. Transfer cake to prepared cardboard base, using a bit of glaze or white buttercream to secure it in place.

## Preparing the frosting

1 recipe Classic Buttercream

Paste food colors: sky blue, leaf green, orange sherbet, pink, lemon yellow, lavender, black

Tubes: 1, 2, 6, 11

6 decorating bags, fitted with couplings

1 parchment cone

1. Measure ¼ cup of buttercream into each of six small bowls. Tint blue, green, orange, pink, yellow and dark gray, which will turn black when it dries.
2. Insert tube 1 into a parchment cone; fill with dark gray.
3. Transfer remaining tinted buttercreams into five decorating bags; place a small piece of waxed paper over each open coupling to prevent the buttercream from crusting at the opening. (Remove paper before attaching tube to coupling.)
4. Tint ¾ cup buttercream lavender; transfer to a decorating bag and cover open coupling with waxed paper.
5. Cover remaining white buttercream with plastic wrap.
6. Set aside remaining equipment.

## Decorating the cake

1. Frost top and sides of cake with white buttercream, spreading it as smoothly as possible.
2. Attach tube 2 to bag of orange; pipe message.
3. The round balloons are formed by piping a coil with tube 11 and then smoothing it over with a small heated spatula. Using the photograph as a guide to placement, pipe balloons in each color on the surface of the cake.
4. The lips of the balloons are piped with tube 2, using a back and forth motion.
5. Using tube 1 dark gray, pipe names and strings attached to balloons, then outline balloons at bottom of cake.
6. Attach tube 6 to bag of lavender; pipe border around top of cake.

# Sweet Sixteen Cake

**Sweet sixteen and she's growing up. The cake is decorated with roses to wish her love, ruffles to wish her the finest things in life, and pearls to wish her wisdom. Notice that the top edge of the cake is beveled for a softer shape and that the lettering is accented with tiny dots to give it a delicate look. Practice ruffles on an inverted cake pan to determine the depth of each garland; use a garland marker to mark the *top* edge of each ruffle.**

## Preparing the cake

*2 9-inch round cake layers, cooled to room temperature and leveled*

*1 recipe Jam Glaze*

*1 9-inch round cardboard base, covered with parchment*

**1.** Using a sharp serrated knife, bevel the top edge of one cake layer.

**2.** Place cake layers on a rack; brush on warm jam glaze, then air-dry for about an hour to allow glaze to set.

**3.** Transfer unbeveled cake layer to the prepared cardboard base using a bit of glaze or buttercream to secure it in place. Spread a thin layer of white buttercream over the top, then position beveled layer (beveled edge on top) over the first.

## Preparing the frosting

*1 recipe Classic Buttercream*

*Paste food colors: pink, leaf green, lemon yellow*

Mix and tint buttercream the day before or while waiting for the glaze to set.

**1.** Place ¼ cup buttercream into a small bowl and tint it pale leaf green; cover with plastic wrap.

**2.** Place ¼ cup buttercream into a small bowl and tint it yellow; cover with plastic wrap.

**3.** Place about a third of the remaining buttercream into a bowl and tint it pink; cover with plastic wrap. Cover remaining white buttercream with plastic wrap.

## Decorating the cake

*Tubes: 2, 4, 10, 65s, 66, 104, 225*

*Flower nail*

*Garland marker*

*3 decorating bags, fitted with couplings*

*1 parchment cone*

**1.** Frost the sides and top of the cake with white buttercream. Go over the frosted area with a hot spatula to make it as smooth as possible.

**2.** Measure and mark six garlands on side of cake.

**3.** Fill a decorating bag with white buttercream; attach tube 10. Pipe beaded border around cake base.

**4.** Fill another decorating bag with pink buttercream; attach tube 104. Using flower nail, pipe two pink roses and place them in the freezer to harden.

**5.** Continuing with tube 104, pipe ruffled garlands with wide end of tube touching cake and narrow end tilted outward.

**6.** Fit tube 4 to the bag of white buttercream; pipe strings of beads directly over the pink garlands.

**7.** Remove roses from freezer and position on top of cake.

**8.** Fit tube 225 to the bag of pink buttercream and pipe drop flowers on top of cake to accent the roses. Pipe clusters of three drop flowers above the peak of each garland on the side of the cake. Fit tube 2 to the bag of pink buttercream; write message, then pipe pink dots on top of cake to accent the drop flowers and lettering. Wash and dry tube 2.

**9.** Place green buttercream in a decorating bag fitted with tube 65s. Pipe tiny leaves adjacent to the drop flowers on top and side of cake. Change to tube 66; pipe leaves for roses.

**10.** Place tube 2 into the parchment cone and fill with yellow buttercream. Pipe a yellow dot in the center of each drop flower.

# Sled Cake

Intensify the excitement of a winter snowfall with this easy to decorate sled cake. Those who have been traveling, working or playing in the drifts will welcome the warmth of a kitchen filled with the aroma of freshly baked cake and a steaming cup of cocoa or coffee.

Or, pipe the name "Rosebud" in one corner of the sled and present it as a birthday cake to a movie-trivia buff. See if they recall that just such a sled played a major role in the film Citizen Kane, starring Orson Welles.

Another obvious use for this realistic-looking sled cake is a child's birthday party in the winter months. But, sometimes it is even more fun to do the unexpected—present it as dessert on a warm summer night, and no doubt, everyone will think cool.

## Preparing the cake and patterns

*1 9- by 13-inch cake layer, cooled to room temperature and leveled*

*1 recipe Jam Glaze*

*9- by 13-inch cardboard base, covered with parchment*

1. Place cake on a rack. Brush on warm jam glaze, then air-dry for about an hour or until set.
2. Using diagram as a guide, draw a pattern for the top and sides of the sled on parchment or waxed paper.
3. Transfer cake to prepared cardboard base, using a bit of jam glaze or buttercream to secure it in place.

## Preparing the frosting

*1 recipe Classic Buttercream*

*3 tablespoons unsweetened cocoa*

*1 tablespoon butter, softened*

*2 teaspoons milk*

*Paste food colors: super Christmas red, egg yellow, malt brown*

*Tubes: 4, 6, 16, 18, 48*

*3 decorating bags, fitted with couplings*

*1 parchment cone*

1. Place ¾ cup buttercream into a bowl. Add cocoa, butter and milk, beating until smooth and fluffy. Insert tube 6 into a parchment cone; fill with chocolate buttercream.

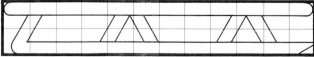

**TOP EDGE OF CAKE**

**EACH SQUARE EQUALS 1 INCH**

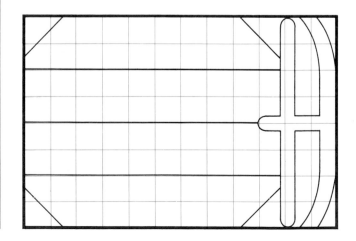

**2.** Tint 1 cup buttercream red. Transfer to a decorating bag fitted with tube 4.

**3.** Using egg yellow and malt brown, tint 1½ cups buttercream tan. Transfer to a decorating bag fitted with tube 48.

**4.** Cover remaining white buttercream with plastic wrap.

## Decorating the cake

**1.** Frost sides of cake white, spreading buttercream as smoothly as possible.

**2.** Place pattern on top of cake. Mark design by punching small holes through the paper and into the cake with a toothpick. When sides of cake have crusted, use toothpick to mark pattern for runners on sides of cake.

**3.** Outline red portions of cake with tube 4. Attach tube 18 to bag of red; pipe stars to fill in red outlines.

**4.** Using tube 48 with serrated side up, pipe tan lines on top of cake. Remove excess tan from corners with a sharp knife.

**5.** Pipe tube 6 chocolate lines within and to outline the tan area.

**6.** Attach tube 16 to a decorating bag and fill with white buttercream. Pipe stars on sides of cake to resemble snowflakes. Pipe stars to fill in white area on top of cake and to border the front and back of the cake.

**7.** Transfer cake to serving platter of your choice; relax and have a (snow) ball.

# Ballet Dancer Cake

Surprise a ballerina with a special cake on her birthday. This one is decorated with pink and lavender, but the color scheme can easily be changed to match her favorite slippers and leotards. If she is a chocolate lover, you might substitute chocolate buttercream for the lavender trim, leaving the pink as is. A chocolate, white and blue color scheme, on the other hand, could be used to honor a male dancer, and in this case, it would be more appropriate to omit the tiny dots adorning the slippers.

## Preparing the cake and patterns

*1 9- by 13-inch cake layer, cooled to room temperature and leveled*

*1 recipe Jam Glaze*

*9- by 13-inch cardboard base, covered with parchment*

**1.** Place cake on a rack; brush on warm jam glaze and air-dry for about an hour, until set.
**2.** Transfer cake to prepared cardboard base, using a bit of glaze or buttercream to secure in place.

**3.** Trace patterns for feet onto parchment or waxed paper; cut out patterns.

## Preparing the frosting

*1 recipe Classic Buttercream*

*Paste food colors: pink, lavender or violet*

*Tubes: 1, 2, 3, 6, 18*

*2 decorating bags, fitted with couplings*

*1 parchment cone*

Mix and tint buttercream while waiting for the glaze to set.

**1.** Tint 1¼ cups buttercream pink. Place in a decorating bag fitted with tube 6.
**2.** Tint 1¼ cups buttercream a medium shade of lavender. Place in a decorating bag fitted with tube 3.
**3.** Tint ¼ cup buttercream pale lavender. Insert tube 2 into a parchment cone; fill with pale lavender.
**4.** Cover remaining white buttercream with plastic wrap.

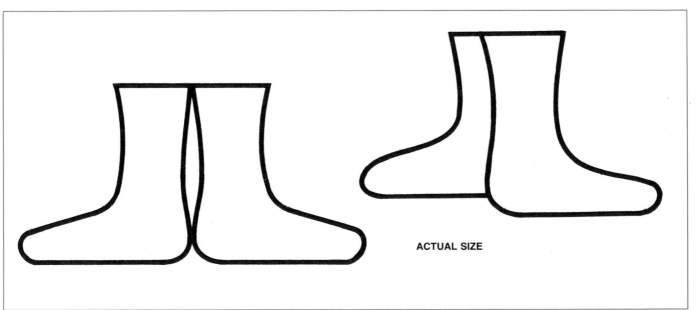

**ACTUAL SIZE**

## Decorating the Cake

**1.** Frost top and sides of cake with white butter-cream, spreading it as smoothly as possible.

**2.** Measure cake and use a spatula to mark horizontal lines across the top of the cake. (The spaces provided for the words should measure about 1-inch; the spaces provided for the feet should measure about 2¼-inches.) Pipe tube 3 lavender lines along the marks.

**3.** Place feet patterns on cake; outline with toothpick marks. Pipe outline of feet and fill in with tube 6 pink. Smooth surface of feet with a small heated spatula.

**4.** Pipe tube 2 pale lavender laces on slippers.

**5.** Pipe message with tube 3 darker lavender. Attach tube 1 to bag of darker lavender; pipe dots on slippers. Attach tube 6 to bag of darker lavender; pipe outline on top of cake.

**6.** Attach tube 18 to bag of pink; pipe shell border arond top of cake.

**7.** Transfer cake to serving platter of your choice. Pipe a tube 6 darker lavender caulking line around base of cake.

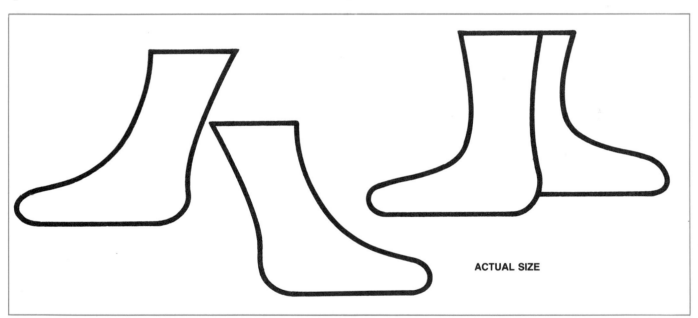

**ACTUAL SIZE**

# Romantic Cakes

WEDDING VOW SAMPLER CAKE

SYMPHONY OF FLOWERS
WEDDING CAKE

ALL-OCCASION
CELEBRATION CAKE

ANNIVERSARY WALTZ CAKE

LOVING HEART
ENGAGEMENT CAKE

# Wedding Vow Sampler Cake

A beautiful linen sampler stitched with love provides an ideal motif for a wedding or anniversary cake. Most of the decoration is piped with tube 1, which requires a steady hand and a good deal of patience, but the flowers and leaves as well as the tube 2 hearts are made in advance with royal icing.

Powdered red food coloring is used instead of paste because it tints to a lovely shade of strawberry red in keeping with the soft color tone of the cake. Keep in mind that powdered colors darken quite a bit when they dry, and the final red used here is made by tinting only to a medium shade of pink.

## Preparing the decorations

*1 recipe Royal Icing*

*Powdered food color: red*

*Paste food colors: orange, violet, moss green, egg yellow*

*Tubes: 1, 2*

*8 parchment cones*

Try to select a cool, dry day to work with Royal Icing. Mix the icing to a very stiff consistency.

**1.** First mix the colors. (Keep bowl of Royal Icing covered with a damp paper towel as you work.) Using powdered red, tint 1 cup icing strawberry pink, which will dry to a soft red. Place 2 tablespoons of the strawberry pink icing into a small bowl and mix with 2 tablespoons white icing to make a lighter pink shade. Cover bowls with damp paper towels and refrigerate.

Place ¼ cup icing into each of three small bowls. Using paste colors, tint pale moss green, medium moss green, and egg yellow. Cover bowls with damp paper towels and refrigerate.

Using orange and just a bit of violet, tint ⅓ cup icing burnt orange. Place 2 tablespoons of the burnt orange into a small bowl and mix with 2 tablespoons white icing to make a pale shade of melon. Cover bowls with damp paper towels and refrigerate.

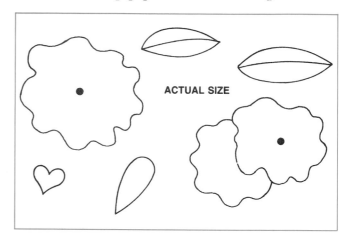

**ACTUAL SIZE**

**2.** Trace patterns for flowers, leaves and heart onto parchment paper. Place a sheet of waxed paper over the patterns—the decorations will be piped onto the waxed paper following the design of the patterns that show through underneath. With each decoration that you pipe, simply maneuver the pattern below so that it shows through on a fresh space of the waxed paper.

**3.** To make crewel stitched flowers, fill in pattern by piping tight lines with tube 1 and working from the edge of the petal toward the center. Begin each line with a slightly mounded dot before pulling it inward. Change colors as necessary, and pipe a few tube 1 yellow dots in the center of each flower. The buds are formed by piping row upon row of short lines, each beginning with a slightly mounded dot.

**4.** To make crewel stitched leaves, fill in pattern by piping short, tight lines with tube 1 and working from the edge of the leaf toward the center. Begin each line with a slightly mounded dot before pulling it inward. Pipe the leaves in two shades of green. The central vein is formed by piping a trail of tube 1 beading.

**5.** To make hearts, fill in pattern by piping two shells with tube 2. To make the work go faster, pipe one heart to serve as a model, and then place a sheet of lined paper underneath the waxed paper so that the first heart is positioned at the beginning of a line.

Pipe hearts of similar size along the line. You will need at least 34 hearts in all.

Air-dry decorations overnight, then transfer the sheets of waxed paper to a covered box and store at room temperature until needed.

## Preparing the frosting

*1 recipe Classic Buttercream*

*Paste food colors: orange, violet, moss green, malt brown, egg yellow*

Mix and tint buttercream the day before frosting the cake. Because brown food color is composed of many colors, each color particle is absorbed by the fat in the frosting at a different rate. It takes several hours for all the coloring matter to dissolve completely. When first mixed, you may even notice tiny flecks of the different colors in the buttercream. Rebeat frosting the following day, and it will then turn into a nice solid color.

**1.** Using orange and just a bit of violet, tint 1 cup buttercream burnt orange. Cover with plastic wrap and store in refrigerator. Sitr before using.

**2.** Tint ½ cup buttercream moss green; cover with plastic wrap and store in the refrigerator. Stir before using.

**3.** Using malt brown and a bit of egg yellow, tint remaining buttercream light beige. Cover with plastic wrap and store in the refrigerator. Beat again before using.

## Preparing the cake

*1 9- by 13-inch cake layer, cooled to room temperature and leveled*

*1 recipe Jam Glaze*

*9- by 13-inch cardboard base, covered with parchment*

**1.** Place cake on rack. Brush on warm jam glaze, then air-dry for about an hour or until set.

**2.** Transfer cake to prepared cardboard base, using a bit of jam glaze or buttercream to secure it in place.

## Decorating the cake

*Tubes: 1, 2, 6*

*1 decorating bag, fitted with a coupling*

*2 parchment cones*

**1.** Frost top and sides of cake with a smooth layer of beige buttercream.

**2.** Transfer green buttercream to a parchment cone fitted with tube 1. Pipe top row of lettering with tiny tube 1 x's, then finish piping wedding vow in the normal manner. Pipe tube 1 dots at end of message.

**3.** Insert tube 6 into a parchment cone and fill with beige buttercream. Pipe a line to frame the wedding vow. Pipe tube 1 green x's over the beige line.

**4.** Attach tube 2 to a decorating bag and fill with orange. Pipe inner border line, allowing about 1" from the edge of the cake.

**5.** Position flowers on cake. Pipe a trail of tube 1 green beading to make the stems. Arrange buds and leaves along stems. Pipe short tube 1 lines to attach stems to buds.

**6.** Position hearts on cake, inverting one after the other. Pipe tube 2 orange dots, inverting their positions, in between the hearts.

**7.** Wash and dry tube 6; attach to bag of orange. Pipe border around top edge of cake. Transfer cake to serving platter of your choice. Pipe a tube 6 orange caulking line around base of cake.

# Symphony of Flowers Wedding Cake

Don't be daunted by the cascades of flowers adorning this three-tier wedding cake. The roses, of course, require time and practice, but shouldn't present a problem since they can be made in advance and refrigerated. The other flowers are piped directly onto the cake, using drop-flower tubes which require only one squeeze of the decorating bag to form perfect petal arrangements.

Actually, decorating a wedding cake is not the herculean task that it would seem to be, provided the project is approached one step at a time. A three-day countdown is outlined below.

## Day 1: preparing the cake

*Three-tier Gold or Silver Cake (see recipe on page 49)*

*2 recipes Jam Glaze*

1. Bake cake layers; cool on racks, level layers.
2. Brush warm jam glaze over each layer, then air-dry for about an hour or until set. Loosely cover with plastic wrap, then store at room temperature or refrigerate, if desired, overnight.

## Day 2: preparing the frosting

*2½ batches Classic Buttercream*

*Paste food colors: egg yellow, pink, moss green*

1. Mix 1½ batches Classic Buttercream together; tint ivory by mixing in a very small amount of egg yellow. Cover with plastic wrap and set aside.
2. Mix an additional recipe Classic Buttercream. Tint ½ cup pale moss green; cover with plastic wrap and refrigerate. Divide remaining white buttercream among three bowls. Tint one bowl pale ivory, one bowl medium egg yellow, and one bowl peach (egg yellow and pink). Cover each with plastic wrap and refrigerate.

## Day 2: preparing the roses

*1 recipe Bette's Decoration Buttercream*

*Paste food color: egg yellow*

*Tubes: 103, 104, 124, 125*

*3 decorating bags*

*2 couplings*

*Flower nail*

1. Mix recipe for Bette's Decoration Buttercream. Tint the entire batch a pale egg yellow. Transfer half the tinted buttercream to another bowl; tint a deeper shade of egg yellow. Cover both bowls with plastic wrap.
2. First make the rose buds. You will need about twelve. Fill a decorating bag with pale yellow; attach tube 104. Fill another decorating bag with deeper yellow; attach tube 103. Fill a third bag with deeper yellow, but do not attach a tube to the coupling. Pipe buds, using the bag with the open coupling to form the mounded base, tube 103 deep yellow centers, and tube 104 pale yellow outer petals. Air-dry buds for several hours, then refrigerate overnight.
3. Remove tubes, buttercream and couplings from two decorating bags. To make roses, insert tube 124 into the bag that contained the deeper yellow; refill bag. Insert tube 125 into the bag that contained the pale yellow; refill bag. Refill and use the bag with the open coupling to form the mounded base of each flower. Pipe 16 more roses with deep yellow centers and pale yellow outer petals. Air-dry roses several hours, then refrigerate overnight.

## Day 2: filling the cake layers

*1 12-inch round cardboard base, double thickness, covered with parchment*

*1 9-inch round cardboard base, uncovered*

*1 6-inch round cardboard base, uncovered*

1. Transfer one cake layer of each size to its appropriate cardboard base; use a small amount of ivory buttercream to secure them in place.

2. Spread a layer of ivory buttercream over the top of each mounted layer and position second layer on top of first.

3. Cover each tier loosely with plastic wrap. Store at room temperature or refrigerate, if desired, overnight. Refrigerate remaining ivory buttercream.

## Day 3: assembling the cake

*14 plastic drinking straws*

*A sturdy 18-inch round serving platter*

1. Frost top and sides of each tier with ivory buttercream, spreading it as smoothly as possible.

2. To assemble the cake, plastic drinking straws must be cut to the exact height of each tier to support the weight of the tiers once they are stacked upon each other. The 12-inch tier has 8 straw supports. Insert four straws two inches from the outer edge of the cake at 12, 3, 6, and 9 o'clock. Make a pencil mark around the straws where they meet the top of the frosting. Remove straws; determine which has the lowest pencil mark, and cut just slightly below the mark. Line up the three other straws, plus four additional straws and cut them all the same length as the first. Replace cut straws at 12, 3, 6 and 9 o'clock, then insert the other four straws equidistant between them. Repeat procedure for 9-inch layer, placing 6 straw supports at 12, 2, 4, 6, 8 and 10 o'clock. Be sure that they are inserted 2 inches from the outer edge of the cake so that they won't show once the tiers are stacked.

3. Transfer 12-inch tier to serving platter, using a small amount of ivory buttercream to secure it in place. Position the 9-inch tier on top of the 12-inch tier so that the 9-inch cardboard base covers the straw supports inserted in the 12-inch tier. Position the 6-inch tier in a like manner, on top of the 9-inch tier.

## Day 3: decorating the cake

*Tubes: 1, 2, 13, 30, 66 (optional), 146, 191, 225*

*3 decorating bags, fitted with couplings*

*1 parchment cone*

1. Attach tube 30 to a decorating bag and fill with ivory buttercream. Pipe a shell border around the base of each tier.

2. Remove buttercream roses and buds from refrigerator. Using ivory buttercream as glue, place the four largest roses on top of the cake at 12, 3, 6, and 9 o'clock. Note that each cascade falls at a curved angle. Position remaining roses on cake, four at the base of each tier, following a curved pattern.

3. The drop flowers are piped at random positions following the curved path of the cascades. Refill decorating bag with ivory buttercream and attach tube 191. Fill another decorating bag with medium yellow and attach tube 225. Fill third bag with peach and attach tube 146. Pipe a few flowers of each color in each of the four cascades.

4. Position rose buds in each of the four cascades.

5. Wash and dry tubes 191, 146, and 225. Attach 191 to bag of medium yellow, 146 to bag of ivory, and 225 to bag of peach. Pipe enough flowers in each color to fill out the cascades.

6. Attach tube 13 to bag of peach; pipe a few tiny flowers wherever needed to balance the arrangement.

7. Dot the tube 13 flowers with tube 1 ivory centers. Dot remaining peach and yellow flowers with tube 2 ivory centers. Dot ivory flowers with tube 2 yellow centers.

8. Transfer green buttercream to a parchment cone cut into the shape of a leaf tube or fitted with tube 66. Pipe leaves sparingly to accent flowers. Congratulations! You have just spent a great deal of time and energy creating this delightful wedding cake, but the result is infinitely more a personal and rewarding than anything you could buy for a once-in-a-lifetime celebration.

# All-Occasion Celebration Cake

Delicate crystallized gladioli add just the right splash of color to this graceful two-tier cake, designed for sophisticated celebrations of all kinds: birthdays and engagements, promotions and retirements, homecomings and farewells. Notice that the top tier is positioned off-center of the bottom tier, in a step-like fashion to enhance the elegant simplicity of the decoration.

For a party of up to twenty-five, bake a standard recipe for white, gold or chocolate cake using one 6-inch and one 9-inch round pan.

For a party of up to fifty, increase the height of the tiers by baking two 6-inch and two 9-inch layers, using the batter recipe for the Three-tier Cake on page 50.

For a party of up to one hundred, add a 12-inch tier, and position both the 6-inch and 9-inch tiers off-center. (Read instructions for Symphony of Flowers Wedding Cake on page 155, to learn how to stack a three-tier cake.) To decorate the 12-inch tier, repeat design of the 9-inch tier.

## Preparing the cake

*1 or 2 6-inch round cake layers, cooled to room temperature and leveled*

*1 or 2 9-inch round cake layers, cooled to room temperature and leveled*

*1 recipe Jam Glaze*

Place cake layers on a rack. Brush on warm jam glaze, then air-dry for about an hour, until set.

## Preparing the frosting

*1 recipe Classic Buttercream*
*Paste food color: moss green*
*Tubes: 65s, 105*

*1 decorating bag, fitted with a coupling*
*1 parchment cone*

Mix and tint buttercream while waiting for glaze to set.

**1.** Tint ¼ cup buttercream moss green. Insert tube 65s into a parchment cone; fill with moss green.

**2.** Attach tube 105 to a decorating bag; fill with white buttercream. Cover remaining white buttercream with plastic wrap.

## Decorating the cake

*Crystallized gladioli, (see instructions, page 58)*

**1.** Fill cake layers with buttercream, if using two for each tier.

**2.** Place 9-inch tier on prepared cardboard base, using a bit of buttercream to secure it in place. Frost top and sides of 9-inch tier with white buttercream, spreading it as smoothly as possible. Transfer to serving platter of your choice.

**3.** Frost top and sides of 6-inch tier with white buttercream, spreading it as smoothly as possible. Place 6-inch tier off-center of the 9-inch tier.

**4.** Using tube 105, pipe white shell border around base of each tier.

**5.** Arrange crystallized flowers on top of tiers, using a dab of buttercream to secure each flower in place.

**6.** Using tube 65s, pipe green ferns to accent flowers.

**Note:** Crystallized gladioli are very fragile and will begin to show noticeable signs of deterioration after 24 hours. If possible, prepare the flowers on the morning that the cake is going to be presented, allowing one hour for preparation and at least two hours drying time.

# Anniversary Waltz Cake

The musical notes on this romantic anniversary cake play, "Tell me I may always dance the anniversary waltz with you." The cake pictured is one 9-inch square layer, which will serve sixteen with a 1- by 4-inch slice. If you'd like to decorate this cake for a larger party, simply bake two 9-inch square layers and place one atop the other, spreading frosting between the layers.

## Preparing the flowers

*1 recipe Bette's Decoration Buttercream*

*Paste food colors: pink, violet, lemon yellow*

*Tubes: 2, 59, 103, 104*

*2 decorating bags, fitted with couplings*

*2 parchment cones*

*Flower nail*

Make flowers the day before you plan to decorate the cake.

**1.** Prepare Bette's Decoration Buttercream. Tint ¼ cup violet; place in parchment cone fitted with tube 59. Tint ¼ cup yellow; place in parchment cone fitted with tube 2. Using a flower nail and tube 59, pipe five or six violets. Pipe two yellow dots in the center of each flower. Place on a tray to air-dry.

**2.** To make two-tone roses and buds, tint 1 cup buttercream a medium shade of pink. Place ¾ cup medium pink into a decorating bag fitted with tube 103. Add remaining ¼ cup of medium pink to remaining white buttercream; stir to mix, but not too thoroughly. Place in decorating bag fitted with tube 104. Using a flower nail, pipe two roses and one rosebud with tube 103 medium pink centers and tube 104 light pink outer petals. Transfer to a tray and air-dry several hours, then refrigerate overnight.

## Preparing the cake

*1 9-inch square cake layer, cooled to room temperature and leveled*

*1 recipe Jam Glaze*

*9-inch square cardboard base, covered with parchment*

**1.** Place cake layer on a rack and brush on warm jam glaze. Allow to set for about an hour.

**2.** Transfer cake to prepared cardboard base using a bit of glaze or buttercream to secure in place. Place on a turntable to decorate.

## Preparing the frosting

*½ recipe Classic Buttercream*
*Paste food colors: pink, violet, green*

*Tubes: 2, 16, 66 (optional)*

*1 decorating bag, fitted with a coupling*

*3 parchment cones*

Mix and tint Classic Buttercream while waiting for glaze to set.

**1.** Tint 1 cup buttercream pink. Fill decorating bag, cover coupling hole with plastic wrap and set bag aside.

**2.** Tint ¼ cup buttercream violet. Transfer to parchment cone fitted with tube 2.

**3.** Tint ¼ cup buttercream green. Transfer to a parchment cone cut into the shape of a small leaf tube or fitted with tube 66.

**4.** Insert tube 16 into a parchment cone and fill with ½ cup white buttercream. Cover remaining buttercream with plastic wrap.

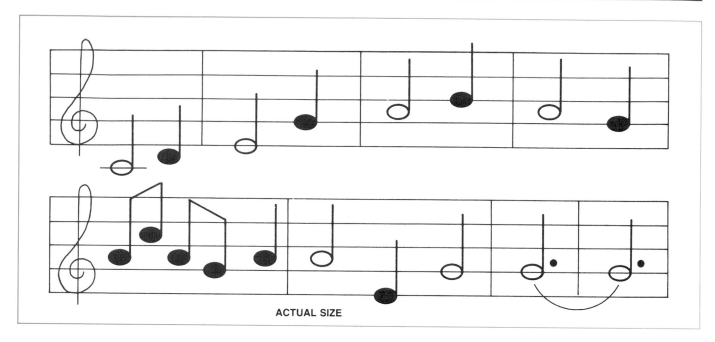

ACTUAL SIZE

## Decorating the cake

**1.** Frost sides and top of cake with white buttercream, spreading as smoothly as possible.

**2.** Using the above pattern, pipe musical staffs in violet with tube 2. Wash and dry tube 2.

**3.** Remove plastic wrap, attach tube 2 to bag of pink. Pipe musical notes, anniversary message and names.

**4.** Arrange flowers on cake. Pipe green leaves to accent flower arrangement.

**5.** Pipe two adjacent rows of tube 16 white lines around upper edge of cake. Wash and dry tube 16.

**6.** Transfer cake to serving platter. Attach tube 16 to bag of pink. Pipe shell border around base of cake.

# Loving Heart Engagement Cake

The background for this cake's decoration is a satiny smooth fondant, or at least that is what it was meant to be. The tiny flaws noticeable on the surface of the cake were caused by the intense heat given off by the studio lamps, and shouldn't occur under normal home-decorating conditions. Frosting the cake with buttercream before covering with fondant will help ensure a flawless alabasterlike surface.

Did you know that you don't need a heart-shaped pan to bake a beautiful heart-shaped cake? The diagrams below illustrate exactly how easy it is to mend a broken heart. Decorate this delicious fantasy whenever love is in the air—for an engagement party, a wedding celebration, an anniversary or even for Valentine's Day.

## Preparing the cake

*1 8-inch round cake layer, cooled to room temperature*

*1 8-inch square cake layer, cooled to room temperature*

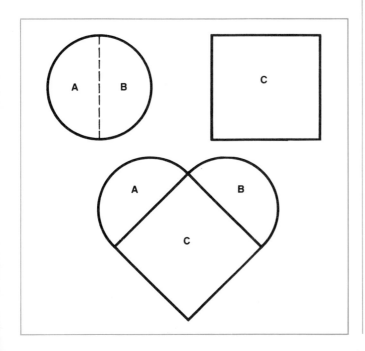

*1 14-inch round or square cardboard cake base, double thickness*

*Parchment paper*

*1 recipe Jam Glaze*

---

1. Cut 8-inch round layer in half as shown in diagram.
2. Assemble heart-shaped cake as shown in diagram; level cake sections and bevel top edge of heart using a sharp knife. Cut cardboard base to size of heart; cover base with parchment; set aside.
3. Disassemble cake parts and transfer them to a cake rack. Brush on warm jam glaze, than air-dry for about an hour or until set.
4. Assemble heart-shaped cake on the prepared cardboard base using a small amount of glaze or white buttercream to hold sections in place.

## Preparing the icing

---

*½ recipe Classic Buttercream*

*1 recipe Quick Fondant Icing*

*Paste food colors: egg yellow, green, pink*

*Tubes: 2, 4, 6, 66 (optional), 103, 104*

*1 decorating bag, fitted with a coupling*

*2 parchment cones*

---

Mix and tint buttercream the day before or while waiting for the glaze to set.

1. Place ½ cup buttercream into a small bowl and tint it pale yellow. Transfer to a parchment cone fitted with tube 103; set aside.
2. Place ¼ cup buttercream into a small bowl and tint it pale green. Transfer to a parchment cone cut into the shape of a leaf tube or fitted with tube 66; set aside.
3. Fill a decorating bag with white buttercream; attach tube 104. Cover remaining white buttercream with plastic wrap.
4. Prepare and tint fondant a delicate pastel pink.
5. Set aside remaining equipment until decorating.

## Decorating the cake

*Flower nail*

1. Frost the sides and top of the cake with a smooth, thin layer of white buttercream. Allow to set for twenty minutes.

2. Make two-tone roses and buds using tube 103 yellow center petals and tube 104 white outer petals. Place in the freezer to harden.

3. Spread warm fondant as evenly as possible over entire cake, piercing air bubbles with a straight pin as soon as they form.

4. Fit tube 2 to the bag of white buttercream; pipe even diagonal rows of seed pearls about ¾ inch apart over the entire surface of the fondant.

5. Fit tube 4 to the bag of white buttercream; write message.

6. Fit tube 6 to the bag of white buttercream; pipe beads around base of cake.

7. Arrange roses on cake. Finish off with a few green leaves to accent the flower arrangement.

# Index

## Cake

## Decorations

# Equipment

# Frostings

# Glazes